Exploring Your
SOLAR SYSTEM

BY ELIZABETH RATHBUN

BOOKS FOR WORLD EXPLORERS
NATIONAL GEOGRAPHIC SOCIETY

Destination: The Solar System

Congratulations! You have graduated at the top of your class from the International Space School. For this achievement, you have won the school's Space Explorer Award. As you know, this award entitles you to take a guided tour of the solar system. You can read about highlights of your upcoming trip on these two pages.

You will carry out your mission aboard the new interplanetary spacecraft *Odyssey*. Experienced astronauts will serve as your crew, and a team of scientific experts will be your guides. You will first travel by space shuttle to the Earth-Orbiting Space Station (EOSS), then board *Odyssey* to continue your journey.

Odyssey has been equipped with the latest computerized navigation system. In *Odyssey*'s observatory, you will use the most sophisticated imaging equipment available. During part of the trip, laser-activated nuclear fusion engines will transport you at one-tenth the speed of light.

All preparations are complete. Please report immediately to your mission command post: Kennedy Space Center, Cape Canaveral, Florida.

SPACE SHUTTLE *ATLANTIS*

1 Countdown to Adventure 4

You'll travel by space shuttle to the Earth-Orbiting Space Station (EOSS), and then board your interplanetary craft. Aboard EOSS, the crew will give you travel tips for space, and scientific experts will brief you on what lies ahead.

◀ *From an interplanetary spacecraft leaving Earth, the Milky Way—home galaxy of the solar system—might look as it does in this artist's view.*

TITLE PAGE: A young astronaut approaching Miranda, a moon of Uranus, gazes at the planet. This imaginary scene may one day happen.

COVER: In a futuristic scene, an engineer mines an asteroid. Earth is visible in the distance, beyond its moon. Asteroids—chunks of rock and metal—may provide resources for use on Earth and in future space colonies.

Copyright © 1989 National Geographic Society
Library of Congress CIP Data: Page 96

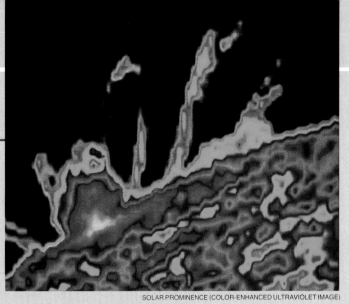
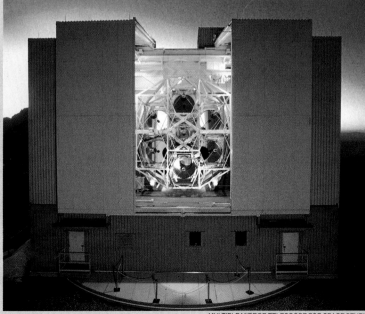

1

Countdown to Adventure

With a roar and a burst of flame, the space shuttle's massive rocket engines ignite. Inside the shuttle's cabin, the noise is shattering. The rockets' thrust forces you deep into your seat, and the spacecraft shudders as it soars into a high arc. Minutes later, the booster rockets and then the fuel tank are jettisoned. You are streaking toward the Earth-Orbiting Space Station (EOSS). You'll arrive within two days. Your space adventure has begun!

A picture (right) on a monitor catches your eye. You see what appear to be colored streetlights shining through fog. Your solar expert explains that what you see is actually a telescopic view of a group of nebulae—clouds of dust and gas. They lie in a distant region called the Rho Ophiuchus (ROH oh-fee-YOU-kus) Dark Cloud. There, stars born in swirling, dusty darkness glow like streetlights. The remains of exploded stars provide some of the raw material for new stars.

*A*bout 4.6 billion years ago, the sun formed in a nebula—perhaps in a region like the Rho Ophiuchus Dark Cloud. Over millions of years, the gas and dust in the nebula became more and more tightly packed, contracting into a dense, spinning disk. Increasing pressure from the tightly packed material caused the matter at the center of the disk to heat up. Eventually, temperatures became so high that nuclear reactions took place. At that moment, the sun was born—a new shining star. When you fly by the sun in your spacecraft *Odyssey*, you will use special instruments to see the sun in action.

The shuttle docks at EOSS. While you wait for the crew to complete a preflight check of *Odyssey*, you go to the EOSS control center for orientation. On the way, you look through a viewport at Earth. From EOSS, orbiting more than 200 miles above Earth's surface, your planet looks huge. But in the control center, you study an illustration (left) that shows how surprisingly small your blue Earth is when compared with some other members of the solar system.

Odyssey's planet expert explains that the planets began forming at the same time as the sun and from the same gas and dust. Different materials in the nebula changed form—from gas to liquid to solid—at different temperatures. Closest to the hot center of the disk where the sun was developing, rock-forming materials and

Traveler's Bulletin

■ Your itinerary is as follows: You will travel by space shuttle to the Earth-Orbiting Space Station (EOSS). Then you will transfer to the interplanetary spacecraft *Odyssey* for the remainder of the tour.

■ Your tour has been scheduled to coincide with maximum sunspot activity, available space at EOSS, and the best possible alignment of the planets for time and fuel efficiency.

■ To make the best possible time between planets, *Odyssey* will accelerate to its top speed: 1/10 the speed of light, or about 70 million miles an hour.

■ *Odyssey* is equipped with a proton shelter for protection against harmful solar radiation.

■ You will not land on the sun or certain of the planets. When you cannot land, you will make observations from *Odyssey* or from a moon, or you will launch a probe.

■ You will have access to *Odyssey*'s galley, fully stocked with freeze-dried food and other essentials.

■ An interplanetary passport is required of all travelers.

◀ *The inner planets—from lower left, Mercury, Venus, Earth, and Mars—are dwarfed by four of the five outer planets—Jupiter, Saturn, Uranus, and Neptune. Pluto, top right, puzzles experts. Unlike neighboring planets, it has a solid surface. All nine planets contain only about one percent of the matter in the solar system. This painting shows their comparative sizes; distances are not to scale.*

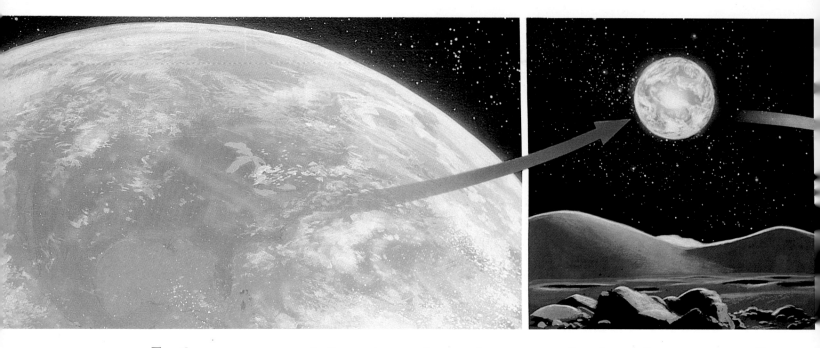

Earth: A Little Planet In a Big Universe

Earth occupies a small corner of an enormous universe. To get an idea of how vast the universe is, imagine moving back from Earth until you are on the far side of the moon—a distance of about 240,000 miles.

From here on the moon, you can still see some of Earth's features: shimmering blue water on the surface and swirling cloud patterns in the atmosphere. Now move back farther, just beyond the orbit of Mars.

metals settled out of the cloud and clumped together. Eventually, these clumps became the rocky inner planets: Mercury, Venus, Earth, and Mars. Farther away, in cooler regions, ice formed and mixed with rocky material. Gradually, these clumps attracted gases and became the four outer planets known as the gas giants: Jupiter, Saturn, Uranus, and Neptune. Exactly how Pluto, the ninth planet, formed is still a mystery.

As you look from Earth to giant Jupiter, the word "big" seems to take on new meaning. But Jupiter, the biggest planet, seems small when you compare it with the sun. The sun swept up 99 percent of the matter in the nebula, the solar expert explains. That left only 1 percent for everything else. But even the sun seems to shrink when you see it in place in its home galaxy—the Milky Way.

The Milky Way is a vast disk of more than *200 billion* stars. The sun lies about a third of the way from the outer edge of that disk. Many stars in the Milky Way Galaxy are smaller than the sun, and many are much larger.

In the universe, distances are so great they are often measured in units called light-years. A light-year is the distance light travels

► From Earth, the Milky Way Galaxy resembles a filmy cloud arcing across the night sky. Dark clouds of dust and gas hide the galaxy's core. The Milky Way is like a huge stellar city. It is the home of the sun and at least 200 billion other stars.

From this point, you can see all the sun's planets. Earth orbits the sun at about 93 million miles. Pluto orbits at an average distance of $3\frac{1}{2}$ billion miles. Now move farther back, to the edge of the Milky Way.

The Milky Way Galaxy is a vast island of stars. The sun, a star of average size, lies about two-thirds of the way out from the center. Its closest neighbor, the star system Alpha Centauri, is about 26 trillion *miles* away!

With another giant move backward, you'll see the Milky Way within its "local group" of galaxies. Not visible are billions of other galaxies. They are separated by the most abundant feature in the universe: empty space.

The Milky Way: Galactic Frisbee

To get an idea of why the Milky Way Galaxy looks as it does from Earth, imagine holding a Frisbee up to your eyes and looking directly at its edge. That's the angle from which observers on Earth view the galaxy. If you could turn the Milky Way on edge, it would look somewhat like a Frisbee. Thin around the edge, it thickens toward the center. The Milky Way even acts like a Frisbee. It spins in space.

Our sun, with its family of planets, moves in an orbit around the center of the galaxy at approximately 140 miles per second. It takes the sun about 230 million years to complete one orbit. In the 4.6 billion years since it formed, the sun has circled the center of the galaxy only 20 times.

9

▼ *Meet an early astronaut, Buck Rogers, from the comic strip that began in 1929. An astronaut is someone who travels, or trains to travel, in space.*

▼ *A pioneer of the U. S. space program, Ham the chimpanzee rocketed 156 miles into space and back in 1961. U. S. space officials observed that Ham suffered no side effects. Three months later, they sent an astronaut into space.*

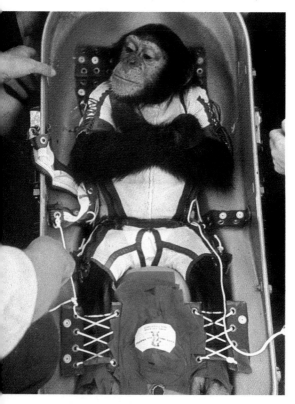

▲ *Since the first manned trip into space in 1961, progress in space has been high-flying, as astronaut Bruce McCandless II shows. Foot restraints hold McCandless in the cargo bay of a space shuttle as it orbits Earth in 1984. He is testing a device for retrieving satellites in space. His space suit supplies oxygen, deflects radiation, and protects him from the extreme temperatures of space.*

through space in one Earth year—about 6 trillion miles. Light takes about *half a day* to streak from one end of the planetary system to the other. To cross the Milky Way, light may take 100,000 years. Trying to imagine all that space is mind-boggling!

The time has come to board *Odyssey*. You take a short break before starting the next phase of your trip. Relaxing, as you have already learned, is easier in a weightless environment. You can move effortlessly. One push, and you're somersaulting across the flight deck. Grab a handhold—or you'll crash into something. Weightlessness can affect you in several ways. You might feel sick for a while. Many astronauts do. Gravity usually pulls blood and other body fluids into the lower body. Without gravity, however, the fluids collect in the upper body, causing unusual sensations. Your body will adjust to its new surroundings. The sickness will soon pass.

Weightlessness will affect your muscles, also. Having little work to do, they will weaken. You'll overcome this by working out in *Odyssey*'s exercise room. You might ride a stationary bike, use a rowing machine, or strap yourself into a treadmill and go for a walk.

Perhaps the biggest problem many astronauts face is being cooped up in a small place with other people for long periods of time. But you are too excited to worry about that. The crew has begun the countdown. *Odyssey*'s solar system tour is now under way!

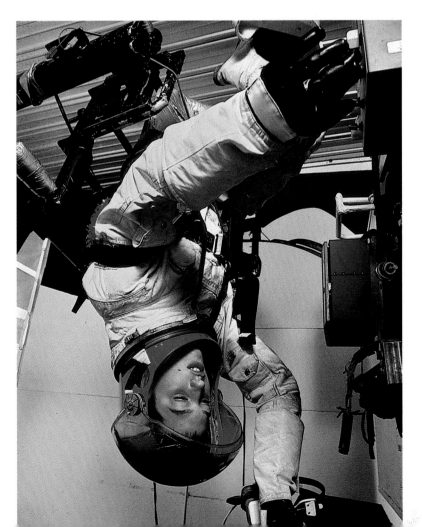

▶ *Space has no up or down, as this boy is finding out at U. S. Space Camp, in Huntsville, Alabama. At the camp, would-be astronauts can practice a space mission using real equipment. This camper is looking for the source of a "radiation leak." A movable seat gives him the feeling of weightlessness he would experience in space.*

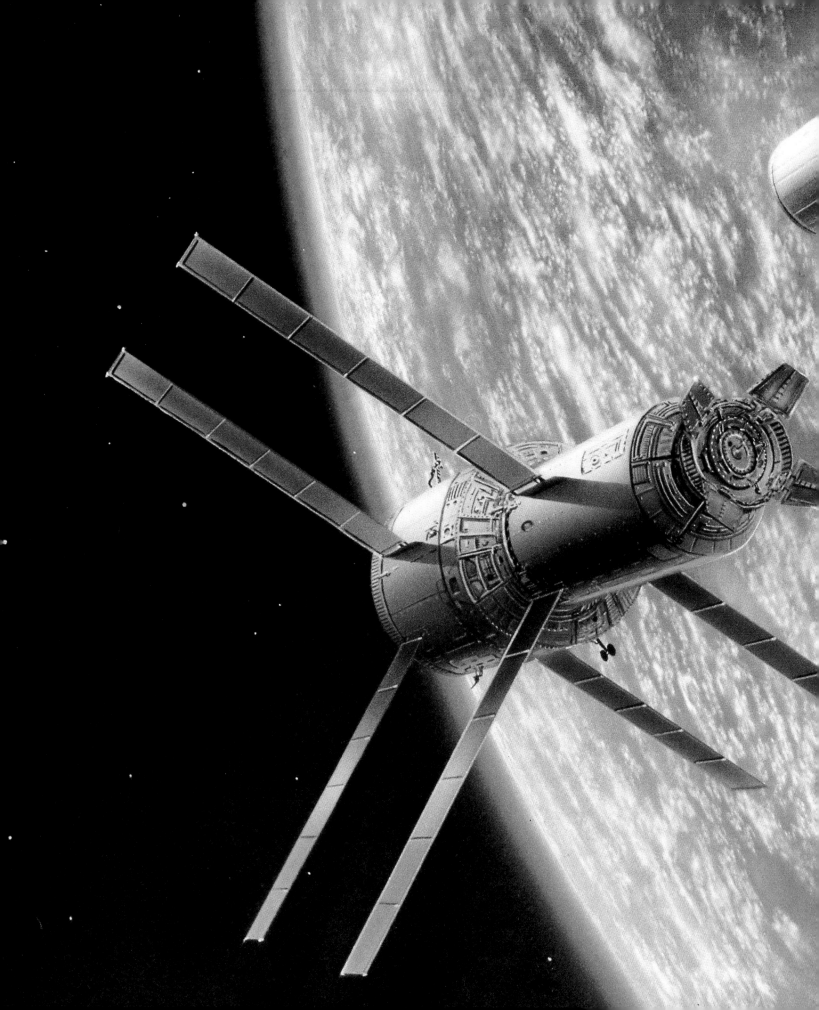

At a space station, *left, orbiting more than 200 miles above Earth, a spacecraft prepares for docking. Stations like the one in this painting might someday be used by travelers to other planets. The space station could be a transfer point for passengers changing from Earth shuttles to interplanetary spacecraft. It could also be a refueling point for interplanetary spacecraft.*

2

Solar Flyby

Zooming toward Mercury, the first stop on your tour, you fly by the sun for a close look at this star—the center of the only known solar system in the universe.

As planned, your solar flyby will coincide with a period of maximum activity on the sun. The increased activity will make your observations more interesting, but it will also increase the danger from high-energy radiation. You'll use specially equipped telescopes to study the sun from the safety of *Odyssey*'s observatory.

The first thing you'll notice is that, without the haze of Earth's atmosphere, the sun looks white, not yellow. The white light comes from the photosphere, the so-called surface layer of gases. When the white light is blocked out by a black disk (right), you can see part of the corona, the sun's outer atmosphere. Computer-added colors in this photograph show different levels of brightness. What a sky show—and it's just beginning!

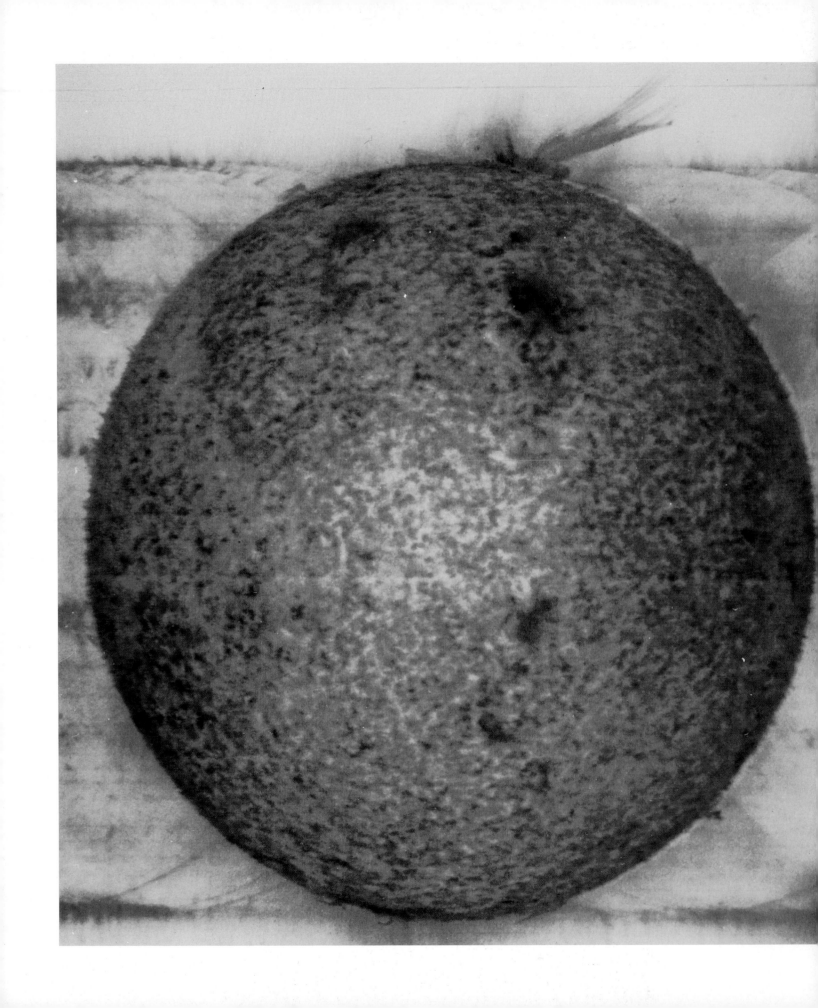

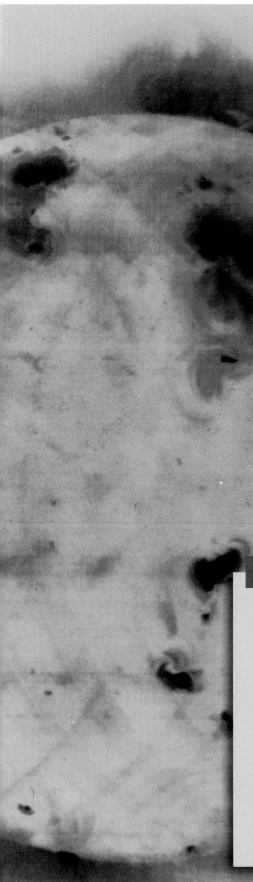

W hen *Odyssey* is about 50 million miles from the sun, the captain slows to cruising speed. This is your chance to observe the boiling, bubbling mass of gases that provide heat and light to planet Earth.

On Earth, even if you were to use the most powerful telescope, you would still get only a limited view of the sun. That's because gases in Earth's atmosphere block certain wavelengths of light coming from the sun. In space, however, you are free of such atmospheric interference. Using specially equipped telescopes, you can see features of the sun you can't see from Earth.

The telescopes on your spacecraft, like those on Skylab (below), are equipped with spectrographs. These are devices that break the sun's light into different wavelengths. With a spectrograph, you can see images of both visible and invisible light.

◀ *A photograph of the sun made from space captures the ultraviolet light normally blocked by Earth's atmosphere. The image reveals an eruption in the chromosphere, a layer of gases above the photosphere. An instrument called a spectrograph made overlapping images of the sun. Several such images show faintly in this picture.*

▶ *Skylab, the first manned space station to study the sun, orbited 270 miles above Earth. In 1973-74, astronauts in Skylab made more than 150,000 images of the sun.*

Traveler's Bulletin

■ The sun is some 93,000,000 miles from Earth. Travel time at light speed— about 8 minutes; at the speed of a 747 jumbo jet—17 years!

■ Sunspots look dark on the sun. But if you could see a typical sunspot in the night sky, it would be 10 times brighter than a full moon.

■ If you could hear the eruptions of columns of gas in the photosphere, they would sound like volcanic explosions. A column erupts about every 8 minutes.

■ If scientists could capture the energy released by a large solar flare, they might be able to use it on Earth. If Earth's energy needs do not increase, the energy from the flare could meet those needs for the next 100,000 years.

■ The force of gravity at the sun's surface is about 28 times stronger than it is at Earth's surface. If you weigh 100 pounds on Earth, you'd weigh about 2,800 pounds— more than a ton—on the sun.

■ The sun produces less heat, pound for pound, than the human body.

CAUTION! DIRECT VIEWING PROHIBITED

OBSERVE PEAK SOLAR ACTIVITY

This painting shows the sun, a ball of gases, as it might look if it were cut open. Scientists think it is made up of layers, like an onion. The core is more than twice the size of Jupiter. In the core, nuclear reactions generate an enormous amount of energy. To reach the surface, where it emerges mainly as visible light, the energy travels as gamma rays and X rays through dense gases in the radiation zone.

In the convection zone, rising columns of gases carry the energy to the surface, or photosphere. This is the only layer of gases normally visible from Earth. The brightness of the photosphere usually hides the sun's outer layers. These include the chromosphere, a region of violent explosions, and the corona, which stretches far into space.

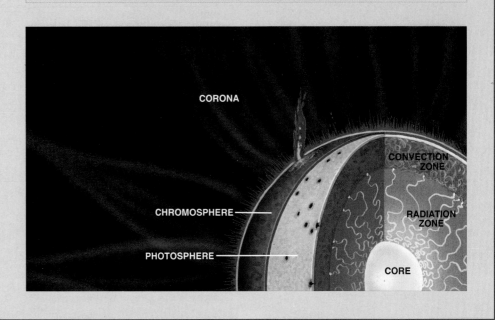

▲ An Indonesian girl catches a solar eclipse in her hands. The bright crescent is the part of the sun not yet covered by the moon. The sun's light shines through a small hole in the thatched roof of her house.

▼ Photographs made at five-minute intervals show the moon as it gradually moves between the Earth and the sun during a solar eclipse. The moon appears black because the side facing the Earth is in shadow.

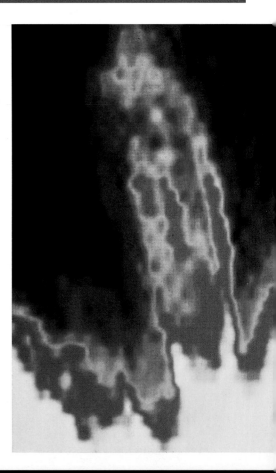

Of course, you must never look directly at the sun. Its light could blind you. Instead, you look at monitors where *Odyssey*'s computers display images of the sun. As you study the images on the monitors, you see clearly that the sun isn't the smooth ball it appears to be from Earth. Its surface is in constant motion.

Odyssey's solar expert tells you that a powerful nuclear furnace in the sun's core creates the energy you see in action. In this furnace, temperature and pressure are so tremendous that, together, they cause nuclear fusion to take place. Tiny particles, the nuclei of hydrogen atoms, smash into each other so hard that they fuse, or combine. Then they form nuclei of helium, a heavier gas. Huge amounts of energy are released in this process.

Hydrogen provides the sun's fuel, and there's enough to last for a long, long time. Scientists estimate that the sun is about 92 percent hydrogen and only about 8 percent helium. They think it has enough fuel to shine for five billion more years!

The energy generated in the core of the sun takes about ten million years to reach the photosphere. The energy must fight its way through dense gases that fill most of the area between the core and

▼ *A filter reveals a violent explosion, called a flare, in the chromosphere. The flare extends upward more than 60,000 miles. The bright areas are regions of hot gases. The dark area beneath the flare is a sunspot in the photosphere.*

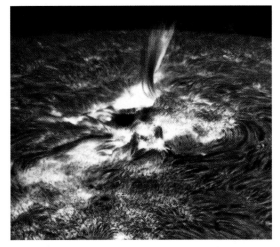

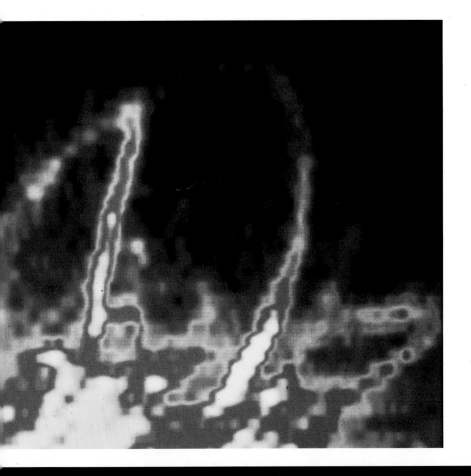

◀ *This view of the sun shows magnetic loops filled with hot gases. They are located in the lower corona, part of the sun's atmosphere. Computer-added colors show differences in brightness.*

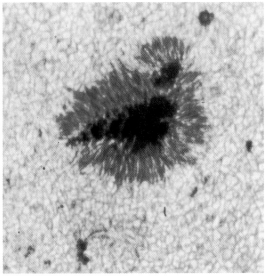

▲ *The large, dark area is a sunspot, a region of strong magnetism in the photosphere. Sunspots appear dark because they are cooler than the gases around them. An increase in sunspots signals an increase in the sun's magnetic activity.*

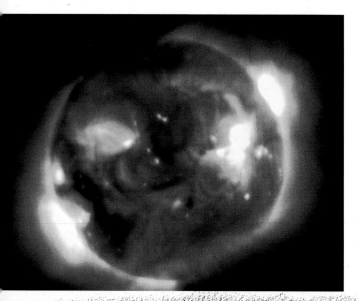

▼ *In an X-ray photograph, the sun's normally invisible corona becomes visible. The dark areas are coronal holes, regions without magnetic loops. The holes allow electrically charged particles called solar wind to escape into space.*

the photosphere. High-energy radiation that began in the core emerges in weaker forms, mainly as waves of visible light. Though the temperature in the core may reach 27,000,000°F, the temperature of the photosphere is a mere 10,000°F.

Long-range solar weather forecasts had predicted increased magnetic activity. Your solar expert explains that the circulation of gases in the sun's interior creates invisible lines of magnetic force. The lines are stretched and twisted, as surface gases along the sun's equator rotate faster than those near its poles. Energy builds up, just as it does in a twisted rubber band. Although there is always magnetic activity on the sun, it reaches a peak about every 11 years.

Your timing is perfect! You are traveling during such a peak period. As you continue to watch the monitors, you see the evidence of greater magnetic activity: numerous sunspots, prominences, and flares. Sunspots are areas of intense magnetism that appear as dark splotches in the photosphere. Prominences—huge, arcing clouds of gases—hang in the outer atmosphere. Flares, the most violent type of solar explosion, shoot out high-speed protons—harmful particles of radiation.

An alarm on *Odyssey* suddenly sounds! This is a warning that an unusually large flare has just erupted. You head for the safety of the proton shelter, a room reinforced against radiation from flares. By the time the all-clear sounds, you are streaking away from the sun. You turn your attention to the next destination, the first planet in the sun's family: Mercury.

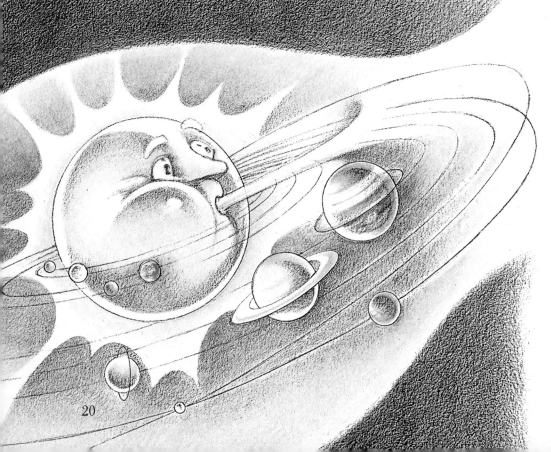

What kind of wind will you never feel?

You will never feel the solar wind. Electrically charged particles that escape from the sun, mostly from coronal holes, make up what scientists call the solar wind. The wind streams out in all directions at speeds of 200 to 500 miles per second. But a magnetic field around Earth protects the planet from the solar wind.

Imagine the sun blowing a bubble around the entire solar system. That bubble is created by the solar wind. It extends far beyond the orbit of Pluto to a region where the solar wind collides with interstellar gases. Scientists don't know exactly where this region is, but they know it marks the outer limit of the sun's influence in space.

When charged particles do get inside Earth's magnetic field, you might see an aurora (uh-ROAR-uh) in the sky, like the one shown (opposite).

Spooky lights of an aurora glow in the sky above a camper's tent in northern Canada. Solar wind particles that penetrate the magnetic field around Earth speed up. They enter Earth's atmosphere, near either the North Pole or the South Pole. Then they collide with gas particles. Energy is released in the form of light, called an aurora.

Solar fireworks display! *This painting shows the violent energy of the sun during a period of peak activity. Hot gases rise to the surface, creating a bubbly network across the photosphere. Jets of gases called spicules form a fiery fringe around the sunspots and along the limb, or edge, of the sun. Glowing gases trapped in magnetic loops arc thousands of miles above the surface.*

3

The Inner Planets

From *Odyssey*'s flight deck, you focus a telescope on each of the four inner planets of the solar system. As planned, you are traveling at a time when the planets are well placed for observation from the spacecraft. You see the inner planets strung out around you: cratered Mercury, bright Venus, blue-and-white Earth, and rusty-looking Mars.

These planets have much in common. All have rocky surfaces wrapped around cores of metal. All are surrounded by atmospheres, or envelopes of gases, though Mercury's atmosphere is so thin that it was discovered only recently.

At right, astronaut Robert L. Stewart floats above the cloud-covered "blue planet." Earth's blue areas indicate that our planet has something the other planets don't have: liquid surface water. Why is Earth different? Perhaps studying the other planets will give you the answer. You'll begin with Mercury.

Mercury

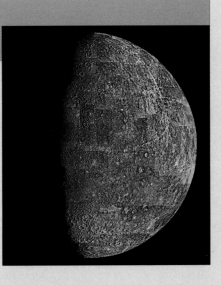

As you approach Mercury, the planet closest to the sun, you almost forget that it *is* a planet. It looks more like Earth's moon. Craters cover most of the surface (right). The largest known crater, called the Caloris Basin, is wider than the state of Texas! The craters formed on Mercury when rocks from space bombarded it. Some of the rocks were bigger than mountains. Comets may also have slammed into the planet. Sometimes the impacts sent material spewing out of the craters to form bright lines called rays. Some of them extend for hundreds of miles.

Scientists think that a period of heavy bombardment occurred early in the history of the solar system. It left craters on all of the inner planets and on Earth's moon. On Earth, wind, water, ice, and other forces erased the craters. But on Mercury, the cratered surface looks much the same as it did three billion years ago.

All aboard! You and several crew members climb into *Odyssey*'s landing

Traveler's Bulletin

■ No matter how loudly you yell on Mercury, your voice can't be heard nearby. Sound cannot travel in the planet's extremely thin atmosphere.

■ Don't look for blue skies over Mercury. Even in daytime, the planet's sky is black. The atmosphere is too thin to scatter light waves.

■ From Mercury, the sun looks about three times as large as it does from Earth.

■ An entire year on Mercury lasts only 88 Earth days. So if you are 10 years old on Earth, you would be age 41½ in Mercury years.

■ If you weigh 100 pounds on Earth, you'd weigh only 38 pounds on Mercury.

■ If you spent one day on Mercury, from certain spots you would be able to see two sunrises and two sunsets.

POSITION LOCATOR

CALORIS BASIN
MERCURY'S HOT SPOT

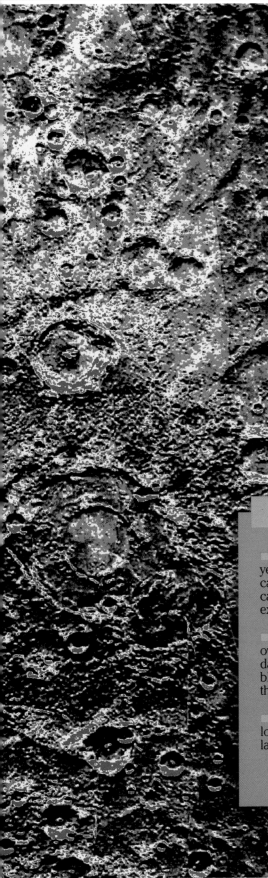

◁ *Like spokes of a wheel, bright lines called rays spread out from craters on Mercury. The rays formed when rocks from space, and possibly comets, hit the planet. A computer added false colors to this photograph.*

▲ *Held close by the sun's gravity, tiny Mercury—the black dot in this photograph—transits, or passes across, the sun's face. Such an event happens about 13 times in every 100 years. The next transit of Mercury will take place in 1993.*

Mercury: Speed champ of the solar system

The name "Mercury" suits the planet. In Roman mythology, Mercury was the swift messenger of the gods. Because the planet lies closest to the sun, it orbits the sun faster than any other planet. Mercury zips along at an average speed of 107,000 miles an hour. That's about one and a half times as fast as Earth's speed around the sun. Mercury circles the sun in just 88 Earth days. But the planet takes 59 Earth days to rotate on its axis. Mercury rotates slowly and revolves quickly. Because of this, and because the planet's orbit takes a more oval than circular path, the sun, when viewed from some spots on Mercury, seems to slow down, stop, then move backward in the sky.

module and head for Mercury. After getting into your space suit, you check the fuel level of the rover, the vehicle that you and the planet expert will use to explore the area near your landing site. The module touches down on Mercury, and the pilot slides the doors open. You steer the rover onto the surface.

You head slowly away from the module, into a lifeless desert. Copper-colored dust and cracked rocks surround you. As you drive across a large crater, the surface ahead suddenly drops off. Inching to the edge of the cliff, you look down and see the rest of the crater more than a mile below. The planet expert explains: This cliff, called a scarp, is one of Mercury's largest. It runs for 310 miles across the surface. Scientists think that scarps formed when Mercury was very young. It may have collided with a huge object, and the force of the impact could have knocked off most of the planet's upper layers. Mercury was left with a thin rocky crust and a huge metal core. Then Mercury cooled, and the large core shrank. The brittle crust buckled and cracked, creating the scarps.

*S*hifting gears in the rover, you turn around and head back to the landing module for the return trip to *Odyssey*. Your suit protected you from outside temperatures. Mercury is the planet with the most extreme temperature changes. At night, temperatures can dip to –274°F. During the day, they can rise to 806°F, hot enough to melt lead! Even though your pilot was careful to land in the twilight zone between day and night, you're relieved to hear that it's time to move on to Venus. But if you think things will cool off there, you're in for a surprise. Venus checks in as the planet with the hottest surface temperature in the solar system.

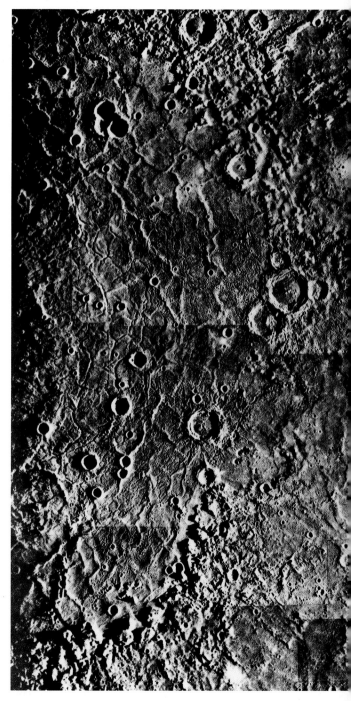

▽ *Like Earth's moon, Mercury shows a face scarred by craters. In the left half of this picture, surface features that stretch from top to bottom form faint patterns of semicircles. The outermost semicircle marks part of the boundary of Mercury's largest known crater, the Caloris Basin. Smaller craters dot the basin, which measures 810 miles across. "Caloris" comes from the Latin word for heat. At certain times during Mercury's orbit, the hottest spot on the planet is near the basin.*

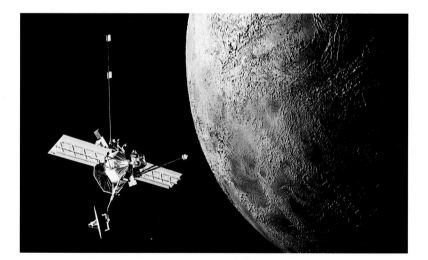

▲ *A painting shows a view of Mariner 10 as it zooms toward the dark side of Mercury. The spacecraft, launched in 1973, photographed half the planet. It made the first closeup images. Before the Mariner mission, Mercury had appeared as a fuzzy blur to Earthbound astronomers.*

Burned by fierce radiation from the sun, Mercury's surface resembles a large, cratered cinder. An artist has painted a view of what the planet might look like if photographed through a spacecraft's viewport. The treated glass of the viewport creates a reddish glare below the sun. From Mercury, you can see features of the sun that are usually not visible from Earth.

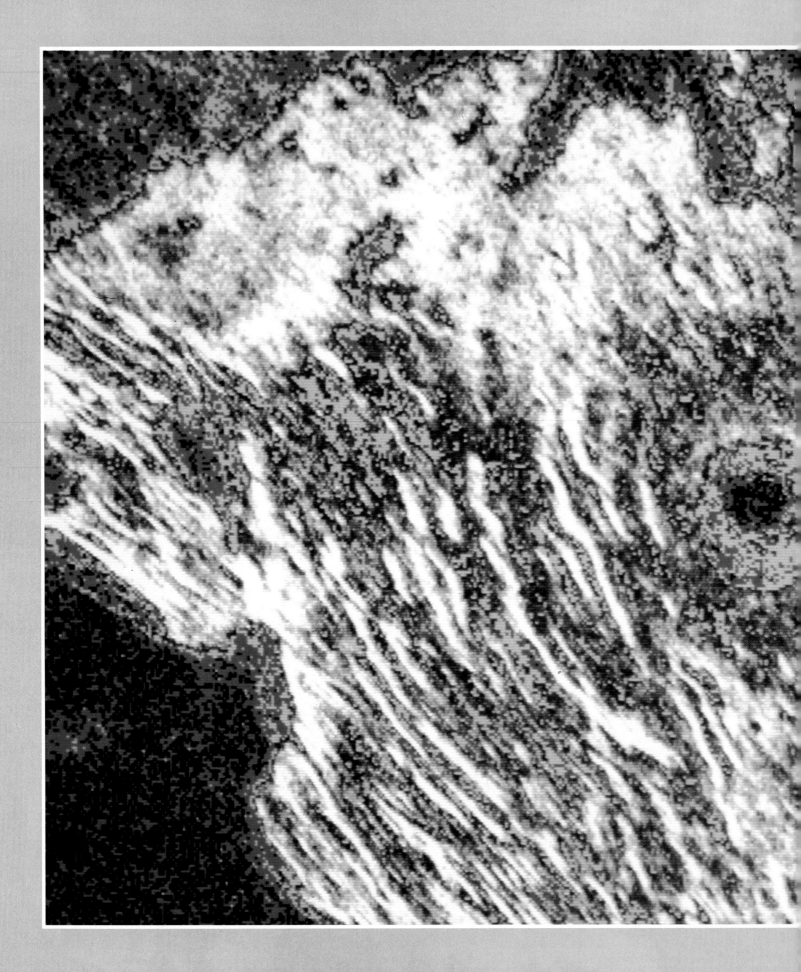

Venus

*T*he yellowish clouds that surround Venus (right) *look* harmless, but they are not. They consist mostly of harsh sulfuric acid. The clouds hide another threat: a bone-dry, superhot surface. You won't attempt to land on the planet. Even if you did, you couldn't leave the landing module to explore. The weight of Venus' atmosphere is crushing. Walking on Venus would feel like walking underwater, more than half a mile beneath the ocean surface on Earth.

Knowing all that, you're happy to study Venus from a safe distance. You deploy *Odyssey*'s radar mapper. It sends out radio waves that bounce off the surface of the planet and back to the mapper. An antenna transmits the waves to *Odyssey*, where a computer translates them into such sharp pictures that you feel as if you were on the planet, studying it close up.

The pictures clearly show that Venus' surface looks like Earth's in many ways. Huge raised areas—some as big as continents on Earth—overlook vast expanses of flat plains. Mountains and volcanoes rise from the

Traveler's Bulletin

■ If you could stand on Venus and see the rising sun through the clouds, it would look flat and stretched into an oval. That's because sunlight bends when it passes through the planet's thick atmosphere.

■ Venus' day is longer than its year. On Venus, a day lasts 243 Earth days; a year, 225 Earth days.

■ Don't expect climate changes on Venus. There's only one kind of climate: hot!

■ The Venusian sky, always overcast, is orange. The planet's thick atmosphere prevents the blue light waves that color Earth's skies from reaching the surface of Venus.

■ About two Earth months pass between sunrise and sunset on Venus.

■ If you weigh 100 pounds on Earth, you'd weigh 91 pounds on Venus.

POSITION LOCATOR

DEPLOY RADAR MAPPER

◁ *Beneath Venus' thick clouds, mountains rise above flat plains. This false-color radar image shows surface textures of a mountain range called Maxwell Montes. Rough ridges appear bright. Smooth valleys appear darker.*

Weather forecast:
Hazy and hot,
no relief in sight.

Some like it hot…but not this hot! On the surface of Venus, the temperature is higher than on any other planet in the solar system—about 900°F. If oceans ever existed on Venus, their waters boiled away long ago.

Carbon dioxide gas makes up most of Venus' atmosphere. The gas traps solar energy, heating the planet. In this way, the carbon dioxide works like glass in a greenhouse. But while plants flourish under glass in a greenhouse on Earth, the "greenhouse effect" on Venus makes the planet too hot and too dry for life.

Besides carbon dioxide, other gases in the atmosphere of Venus also contribute to the greenhouse effect.

34

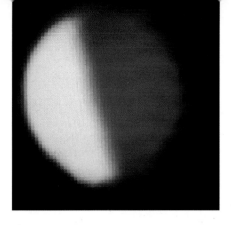

"continents." Some of the mountains may have formed when the rocky crust of Venus shifted and crumpled. The tallest mountain on Venus towers nearly a mile and a half higher than Mount Everest, the tallest mountain on Earth.

Of all the planets, Venus most resembles Earth in size, in mass—how much matter it has, and in density—how tightly the matter is packed. The two planets, however, have many differences. For example, Earth's atmosphere is mostly nitrogen and oxygen, which help make the planet a haven for life. But the Venusian atmosphere consists almost entirely of carbon dioxide, which makes life impossible. That gas traps energy from the sun, making Venus hotter than Mercury. Even at night, Venus doesn't cool much from its high temperature of about 900°F.

Venus checks in as the brightest planet in Earth's sky. Its clouds reflect most of the sun's light. Venus is so bright that people sometimes mistake it for a UFO, or unidentified flying object.

*T*o learn more about Venus, you send a probe into the planet's clouds. They begin about 40 miles above the surface. Winds carry the upper clouds along at more than 200 miles an hour. As the probe descends through the clouds, it detects falling drops of sulfuric acid. But these "raindrops" never reach the surface. In the extreme heat, the drops evaporate. About 20 miles above the surface, the air clears. On Venus, however, clear skies do not mean blue skies. Instead, the planet's sky glows orange from sunrise to sunset, a period that lasts about two Earth months.

The time has come to retrieve the probe and move on. Looking back, you realize that Venus and Earth spin in opposite directions. If you could see the sun from Venus, it would rise in the west and set in the east. It makes you dizzy to imagine a planet spinning backward! You'll welcome the sight of Earth, coming up next.

△ *Viewed from Earth through a heat-sensing infrared telescope, Venus shows a sunlit side and a dark side. On Venus, even the dark night brings no relief from extreme heat.*

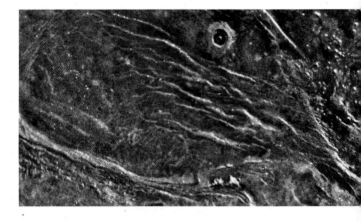

△ *Smooth plains, probably formed by lava flows, cover an area of Venus shown in a recent radar image. Ridges cut across the plains. The ridges may have formed when the crust wrinkled. The circular feature may be an impact crater.*

◁ *In the night sky above Earth, only the moon outshines Venus. Below the moon, Venus glows white, just to the left of a church steeple.*

▷ *In an artist's view, the spacecraft Magellan carries out radar mapping of Venus. The small sphere beyond Venus is Earth. Magellan is scheduled to approach Venus in 1990. It will map most of the planet's surface in fine detail. The radar maps may answer some questions about Venus: Do volcanoes erupt there? Does the planet's surface wrinkle, fold, and split as Earth's does?*

Action, but no life, may characterize the surface of Venus. In this imaginary scene, lightning shatters the skies above an erupting volcano. Clouds of sulfur rise into the thick atmosphere. Hardened lava forms a rugged landscape. Sunlight, scattered by the atmosphere, tints the sky a hazy orange. Scientists have no proof yet that lightning or active volcanoes actually exist on Venus.

Earth

"There's no place like home." You may have said that many times, when talking about your house or hometown. Does the statement also apply to your home planet, Earth (right)? You're about to find out, as you observe Earth from its closest neighbor, the moon.

From *Odyssey*, you and several crew members take off in a landing module and arrive safely at a moon base. You make a few video calls to friends on Earth, then decide to get some well-earned rest before studying Earth and the moon more closely. You head for your sleeping quarters in one of the living modules on the base. The module has no windows. Like all living quarters on the moon, it was built in a shallow trench and covered with a shield of regolith—a mixture of powdery dust and rock fragments. The regolith provides protection from the sun's radiation. You stow your gear inside the module's wall compartments and get settled in your bunk. Although the moon has only one-sixth of Earth's gravity, that gives you enough weight to lie down

Traveler's Bulletin

☐ Earth: It's all wet! Nearly three-fourths of the planet is underwater.

☐ Earth's surface is constantly changing. Large pieces of its thin crust slide on a layer of partly melted rock which lies beneath the crust.

☐ Earth is home to many kinds of life, including human life. Every day, nearly 400,000 people are born on the planet.

☐ Earth's weather occurs in a six-mile-high layer of air that extends from the surface upward. At any moment, in scattered places around Earth, nearly 2,000 thunderstorms are rumbling.

☐ A large satellite—the moon—orbits Earth. The two bodies are sometimes called a double planet.

☐ If you weigh 100 pounds on Earth, you'd weigh only 17 pounds on the moon.

POSITION LOCATOR

FRAGILE
HANDLE WITH CARE

VISIT SEA OF TRANQUILLITY

◁ *In a false-color image of part of North Carolina, you can see what makes Earth different: water and life. The ocean appears mostly black. Square farm plots indicate crops and the presence of intelligent beings who planted them.*

▷ *Salty spray surrounds a bodyboarder riding waves along a beach. Oceans cover nearly 71 percent of Earth's surface. They supply most of the water that evaporates, then falls as rain over the planet's surface.*

▽ *Like all green plants, trees use sunlight, water, and carbon dioxide to make their own food. As they do, they give off oxygen, the gas many other living things must breathe. Without plants, most other life on Earth could not exist. These sequoias grow in California. The largest known sequoia is also the largest living thing on Earth.*

comfortably. Earlier, in *Odyssey*'s weightless environment, you had to strap yourself into a bag attached to the wall to sleep!

You wake up refreshed and ready for a full day of exploration. You slip into your space suit and, along with *Odyssey*'s planet expert, make your way to an observatory on the base. On the way, you can see Earth above the moon's bumpy horizon. Earth looks about four times as large in the sky as the moon does from home. Clouds swirl over the planet's surface.

Through telescopes in the observatory, scientists who work on the base can easily see across more than 200,000 miles of space between the moon and Earth. Aiming a telescope at Earth, you identify blue oceans and brownish red continents. Zooming in for a closer look, you make out mountain ranges, islands, and the Antarctic ice cap. You recall images you have seen of Earth's amazing variety of life: small blades of grass and giant redwood trees; brilliantly colored birds soaring through the air; mammals and reptiles living on the land; and fish swimming in the seas.

Without water, life on Earth could not exist, and could not have developed in the first place. Earth is the only planet with liquid surface water. Most of the living things on Earth—including people— are made up largely of water.

Water hasn't always covered Earth, the planet expert explains. Once, the surface was dry. Early in the planet's history, Earth heated

▽ *Zebras and antelopes called springboks cross a dry grassland in Africa. They are only two of more than a million kinds of animals on Earth. About half a million kinds of plants flourish on our planet.*

As Goldilocks said, "This one's just right!"

If Goldilocks were comparing planets instead of porridge, Venus would be too hot, Mars would be too cold, and Earth would be just right.

Earth's distance from the sun has enabled the planet to keep liquid water on its surface. Such water is necessary for the development of life. Long ago, Venus and Mars may also have had water. Any water on Venus boiled away because of the planet's closeness to the sun and resulting higher temperature. On cold Mars, farther from the sun, water froze. But on mild Earth, the temperature remained "just right." Oceans of water formed and stayed on Earth. Life developed in them.

Smoke, ash, and gases rise from Mount St. Helens, in Washington State, during a 1980 eruption. Throughout most of Earth's history, volcanoes have been changing the surface of the planet. Lava from volcanoes has buried ancient surface features. Volcanic ash has lowered temperatures by blocking out sunlight.

up. That caused gases—mainly water vapor and carbon dioxide—to boil out through volcanoes. As Earth cooled, the water vapor condensed into a thick blanket of clouds. Over millions of years, rain poured down, and oceans formed. With energy from lightning, scientists believe, life-producing organic compounds formed in the atmosphere. The rain washed these compounds into the oceans, where they were protected from the sun's radiation. Icy comets may have added more water when they bombarded Earth early in its history. The comets may have brought organic compounds as well.

Gradually, according to the planet expert, the composition of the envelope of air surrounding Earth changed. Carbon dioxide in the atmosphere dissolved in the oceans. Bacteria and tiny plants called algae grew in ocean water. The algae used the carbon dioxide, light from the sun, and water to manufacture food.

In this process, called photosynthesis, oxygen was released—so much oxygen that it began escaping into the atmosphere. As more plants grew, the oxygen content in the atmosphere increased even more. Some of the oxygen changed chemically, forming a protective shield in the atmosphere called the ozone layer. The layer filtered out much of the sun's deadly radiation and made the land safe for life. Only then could plants and animals survive on land.

Some *Odyssey* crew members join you in the observatory, and you talk about the many things that could upset the delicate balance of Earth's atmosphere. The release of certain chemicals into

▽ *Primitive plants helped create Earth's atmosphere. They released so much oxygen into the air that Earth became suitable for oxygen-breathing animals. Today, plants like these in a Central American rain forest absorb carbon dioxide from the atmosphere and give off oxygen.*

Earth's Complex Cocoon

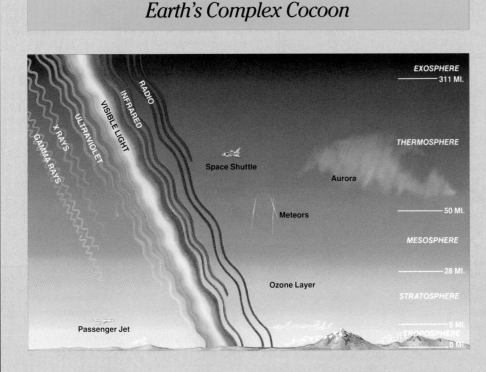

EXOSPHERE
311 MI.

RADIO

INFRARED

VISIBLE LIGHT

ULTRAVIOLET

X RAYS

GAMMA RAYS

THERMOSPHERE

Space Shuttle

Aurora

Meteors

50 MI.

MESOSPHERE

28 MI.

Ozone Layer

STRATOSPHERE

6 MI.

TROPOSPHERE

Passenger Jet

0 MI.

Earth's atmosphere consists of dust and gases—mostly nitrogen and oxygen. Thickest near Earth's surface, the atmosphere gradually thins out as altitude increases. The exosphere *is extremely thin. When energy from the sun, traveling in different wavelengths, passes through the atmosphere, some wavelengths are absorbed. In the* thermosphere—*region of auroras, meteors, and the space shuttle's orbit—gases absorb some ultraviolet waves. Before reaching the* mesosphere, *most gamma rays and X rays are absorbed. In the* stratosphere, *the ozone layer filters out most remaining ultraviolet waves. Visible light and some infrared, radio, and ultraviolet waves penetrate all regions of the atmosphere and reach Earth's surface. Jet aircraft usually fly above the* troposphere—*the region where weather occurs.*

△ In summer, young gardeners in Virginia water newly planted seeds. Fueled by energy from the sun, the seeds will sprout and grow. When these girls enjoy summer in Earth's Northern Hemisphere, children in parts of the Southern Hemisphere are enjoying winter activities.

▷ In winter, skiers in British Columbia, in Canada, race on powdery snow. The tilt of Earth on its axis causes the seasons. Winter arrives in the Northern Hemisphere when the North Pole tilts away from the sun. Summer comes when the North Pole slants toward the sun. The Equator receives direct rays from the sun all the time, and nearby areas have warm weather year-round.

the atmosphere could destroy the protective ozone layer. The burning of fossil fuels—coal, oil, and natural gas—could increase the amounts of carbon dioxide and certain other gases in the atmosphere. That, in turn, could change Earth's climate. You remember the atmosphere that makes Venus such a hot, dry, poisonous, and lifeless planet, and you discuss ways to preserve your own planet as a haven for life.

*B*efore taking off for Mars and the outer planets, you sign up for a walking tour of nearby regions of the moon. Inside the observatory, you had taken off your space suit, but now you put it back on to protect yourself from the noontime heat. It's 273°F outside!

Hiking away from the moon base, you see mostly craters and mountains covered by regolith. It looks like dirty flour. Moving on the moon feels like walking in slow motion on a trampoline. Each step turns into a gleeful bounce. As you bounce, dust rises around your feet. Because the surface of the moon changes so slowly, your footprints may last a million years or more.

Like astronauts before you, you gather small rocks and samples of regolith. The materials that make up the moon resemble those found in Earth's crust. That makes many scientists think the moon might have formed partly from earthly materials. Your planet expert explains the theory. When Earth was very young, a huge object the size of Mars crashed into it. Material from both Earth and the object exploded into space and settled into an orbit around Earth. Eventually, gravity pulled the material together to form the moon.

The period of bombardment early in the life of the solar system

▽ *Earth's natural satellite, the moon is surrounded by the blackness of space. Each time the moon revolves around Earth, it rotates once on its axis. As a result, the same side of the moon—the side you see here—always faces Earth. The far side of the moon was first photographed in 1959 from a spacecraft. Studying those pictures, scientists learned that the far side has many more impact craters than the near side.*

"You're not the only one around here with pull!"

Locked together by gravity, Earth and the moon revolve as partners in space. Earth has more "pull;" it exerts a stronger gravitational force than the moon does because its mass is 81 times as great as the moon's. However, the moon does exert a "pull," or gravitational force, of its own.

Water on the side of Earth facing the moon feels a greater pull than the center of Earth does. Water on this side is pulled toward the moon. The result: high tide. Water on the side of Earth facing away from the moon feels a weaker pull than the center of Earth does. Water on this side is pulled away from the moon. The result: another high tide. As the planet rotates, most coastal areas experience two high tides and two low tides in a period that's just a little longer than a day.

An object as big as Mars slams into Earth.
The collision, many scientists say, may have
happened during Earth's early history and led
to the moon's creation. Perhaps a huge amount
of material exploded into space. Some of the
material settled into an orbit around Earth and
eventually pulled together to form the moon.

Astronaut John Young collects rock samples from the surface of the moon in 1972. The moon is the only natural object in the solar system that humans have visited. The 12 astronauts who reached the moon's surface brought back a total of 841 pounds of lunar rock and regolith for study. Scientists hope to build a moon base someday. They could explore the moon and study stars from telescopes on the base. At night, the moon's sky is four times as dark as Earth's sky. In the absence of any significant lunar atmosphere, the stars appear sharper.

pitted and pocked the moon's surface. Later, melted rock from inside the moon seeped onto the surface and into impact basins, or large craters. The rock covered the bottoms of some and filled others. One impact basin measures about 600 miles across. It would stretch across more than a fifth of the contiguous 48 states.

From Earth, these lava-filled impact basins look somewhat like oceans. Astronomers who first studied them called them "maria" (MAHR-ee-uh), from the Latin word for seas. Maria form patterns on the moon's surface that some people interpret as familiar things—the face of the "man in the moon," for example.

You strap on a rocket pack to ride over one of the largest maria, the Sea of Tranquillity. This is the place where, on July 20, 1969, astronaut Neil Armstrong became the first human to set foot on the moon. His footprints remain, clearly visible.

On your way back to the moon base, you pass a biosphere. Inside this airtight environment, space farmers are growing fruits and vegetables. Next, you pass a mining operation. Miners are collecting regolith. Other workers are extracting minerals from the regolith as part of a process to release oxygen. They use some of the oxygen to make rocket fuel. You will transport enough of this made-on-the-moon fuel back to Odyssey to use during the rest of your journey through the solar system. Stocking up on fuel on the moon is more efficient than carrying, at lift-off, fuel supplies for the entire trip.

It's time to reboard Odyssey and head for Mars, the Red Planet. But first, you take one last look at the blue-and-white marble of Earth, bright against the blackness of space. Is it true that "there's no place like home"? Yes, because only Earth is known to have life. Martians may exist in science fiction, but not in reality. Mars, however, might hold signs of ancient life-forms. Your excitement builds as you take off for your next destination.

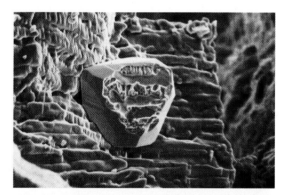

▽ When this sample of lunar material was viewed through a microscope, an iron crystal showed up clearly (center). The crystal formed from vapor when debris thrown out by a meteoroid's impact cooled.

△ Mineral crystals are preserved in a paper-thin slice of volcanic moon rock. By comparing these minerals with those on Earth, scientists can learn more about how the moon—and Earth—formed.

Miners of the future *prepare to board a lunar rover. They have been working in a moon crater. Some have been mining iron ore. Others have been collecting regolith to be used in fuel production and as protective shielding for lunar buildings. Earth is visible beyond the moon's horizon. Although an artist created this imaginary scene, plans already exist for similar mining operations.*

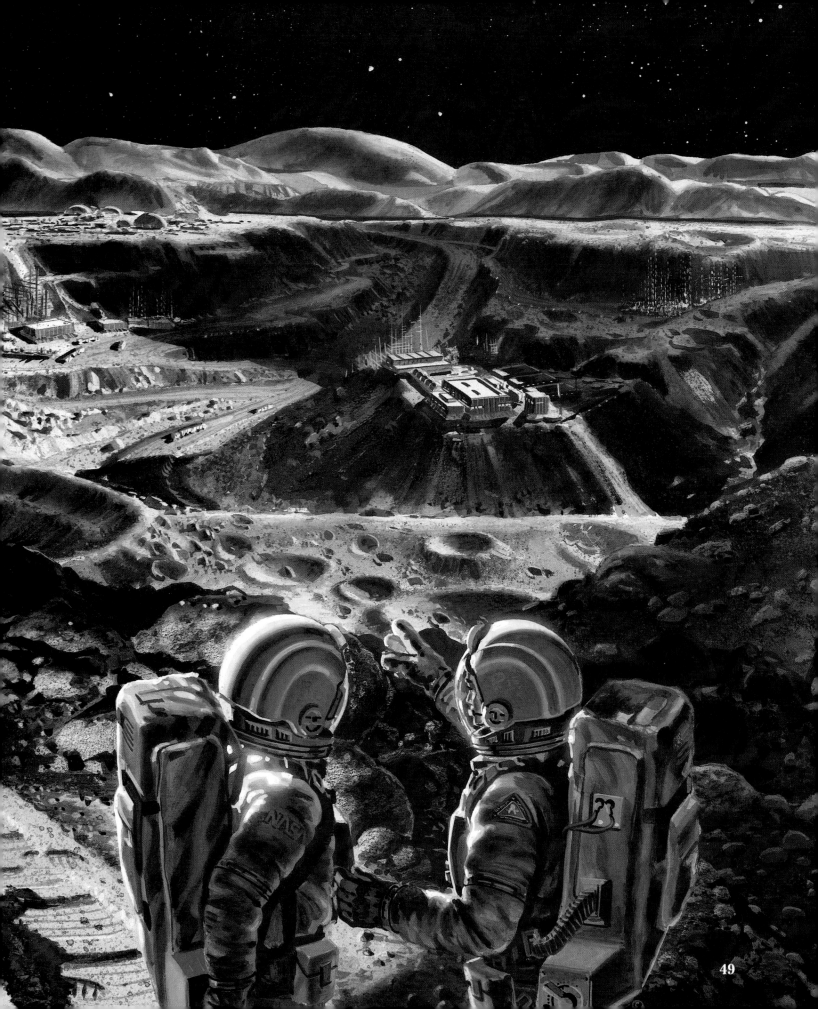

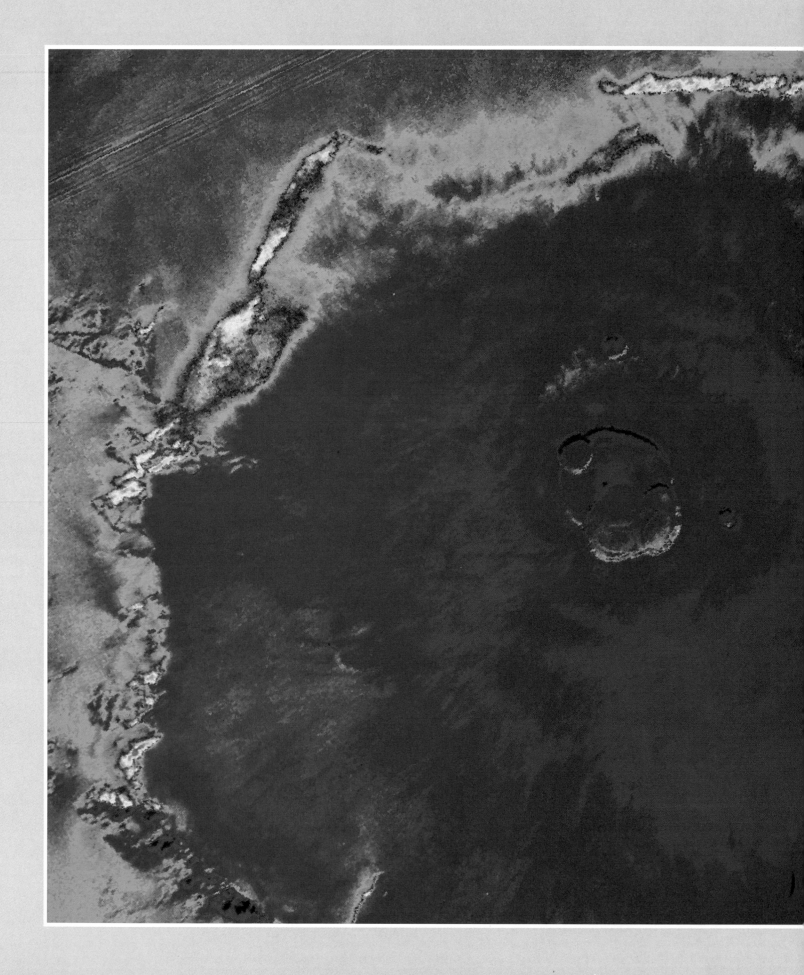

Mars

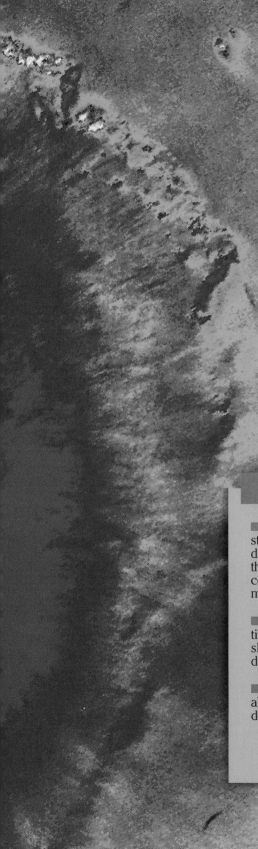

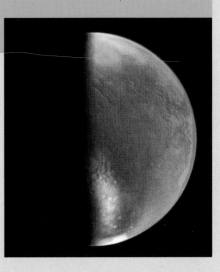

Odyssey is nearing Mars. You peer through a viewport and instantly see why Mars is called the Red Planet. A fine, reddish dust covers the surface. Windblown dust gives the sky a rosy tint. The color of Mars comes from minerals in the soil that contain iron and oxygen.

As your captain maneuvers *Odyssey* closer to Mars, you see that ice covers the planet's south polar region (above right, whitish area at bottom center). Just above this region, frost highlights craters. You see clouds over the far northern regions.

On Mars, huge volcanoes rise from plains. Olympus Mons (left) is the largest volcano—and the largest mountain—known in the solar system. It stands nearly three times as high as Mount Everest, the tallest mountain on Earth. Giant canyons stretch across the surface of Mars. They formed when the surface shifted. They are so big that they make Earth's Grand Canyon look small in comparison! The ice and frost, clouds, volcanoes, and canyons make Mars look more like Earth than any other planet. But there are

Traveler's Bulletin

■ Look out for summer dust storms. Fast winds can whip dust more than 25 miles into the air. A big dust storm can cover the planet and last for months at a time.

■ You'd easily adjust to Mars time. A day on Mars lasts only slightly longer than an Earth day—about 24½ hours.

■ From Mars, the sun looks about two-thirds as large as it does from Earth.

■ You might see something that looks like snow falling on Mars. Carbon dioxide in the atmosphere may freeze around dust, creating "snow" in the planet's polar regions.

■ If you weigh 100 pounds on Earth, you'd weigh 38 pounds on Mars, but only about one and a half ounces on Phobos, one of Mars' two moons.

POSITION LOCATOR

ASTEROID BELT

DUST STORM WATCH

VISIT OLYMPUS MONS

◀ *Largest known volcano in the solar system, Olympus Mons could cover Montana with its base; Rhode Island could fit in its crater. This computer-colored image highlights surface features. Smoother lava appears red.*

important differences. On Earth, for example, the average temperature is 59°F; on Mars, it's much lower, –63°F, a drop of more than 120°. And on Mars the thin atmosphere consists mostly of carbon dioxide, not nitrogen and oxygen.

*I*n spite of the differences between the two planets, scientists consider Mars the second most livable planet. According to *Odyssey*'s planet expert, simple life-forms may have developed in the early days of Mars, when the planet's climate was warmer. Liquid water is essential to life. Today, there is no liquid water on Mars. Almost all water on the planet lies trapped in ice at the poles and frozen in the ground. But in warmer times, water may have flowed on Mars, in places now marked by dry channels. You board a landing module and head for such a channel to search for traces of life.

In the landing module, you put on your space suit. It will keep you warm and provide you with oxygen, since you cannot breathe the carbon dioxide of Mars. The suit will also protect you from the sun's ultraviolet radiation. On Mars, sunlight reaches the surface unchecked by an ozone layer.

Skillfully avoiding several boulders, the pilot lands the module with a gentle thump. As you did on the moon, you drive the rover out of the module and onto the surface. The rugged landscape reminds you of a desert on Earth. You collect samples of soil and rocks from one of the dry channels, and head back to the module and then to *Odyssey*. In the spacecraft's laboratory, you test the samples. Your search for signs of life ends in disappointment. The

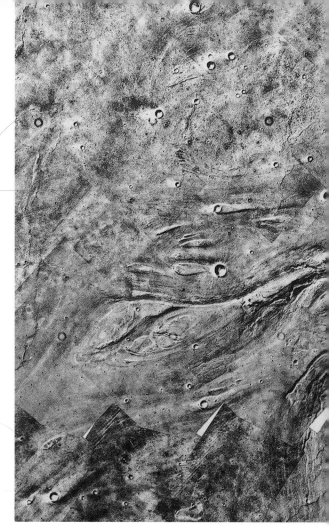

Is truth stranger than science fiction?

No, not really. Strange creatures like these populate science-fiction stories about Mars. Authors of the stories were influenced by some scientists who, as long ago as the late 1700s, stated their belief that Martians existed. Around 1900, astronomer Percival Lowell interpreted some markings on Mars as crops planted along the borders of irrigation canals built by Martians.

But when two Viking probes launched by the United States landed on Mars in 1976, they found no hint of life. Still, the search for life on Mars continues. Perhaps some organic compounds do exist, protected from solar radiation inside cracks in rocks or beneath the Martian soil.

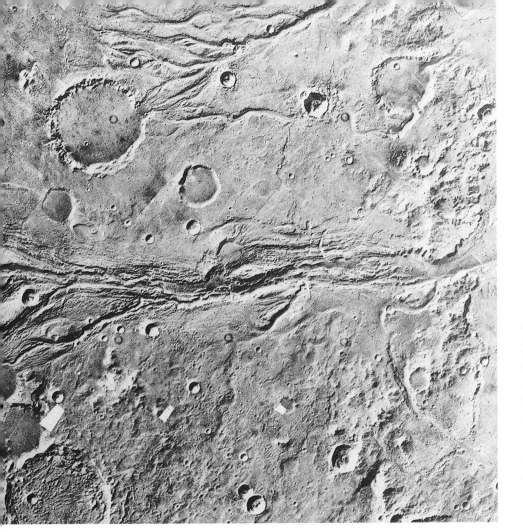

A close-up of the surface of Mars shows channels that may be dry riverbeds. Some scientists believe rushing water once flowed on Mars and cut these channels. If water did flow on Mars, it disappeared long ago. Spots where water collected then may now contain fossil remains of past life.

Early morning fog fills canyons and drifts over plains. The fog shows that some forms of water still exist on Mars. Crystals of water ice make up the fog. Water also lies frozen in the ground and at the poles.

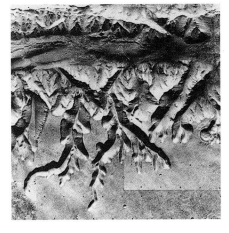

Lakes as big as the Great Lakes may once have existed in these now-empty canyons, called the Valles Marineris. Water and wind may have caused landslides along high cliffs (top). Water and ice may have carved V-shaped valleys (bottom). This photograph shows only part of the Valles Marineris. The main canyons stretch almost a third of the way around Mars.

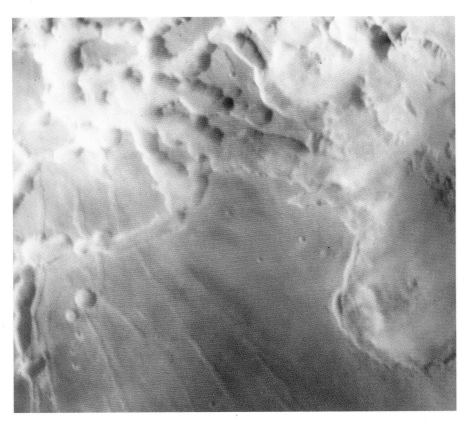

Hopscotch below Mars? In a scene created by an artist, an unmanned Soviet spacecraft releases a "hopper" above Phobos, one of Mars' moons. In the moon's weak gravity, the hopper would be expected to cover about a hundred feet in a single bound. It would record information about the moon each time it touched down.

samples hold no evidence of life. Perhaps future explorers will have better luck, and samples collected from other regions of Mars will yield different results.

Looking through an *Odyssey* viewport, you see Mars' two small, dark moons, Phobos and Deimos. The names come from ancient mythology. Mars was the Roman god of war. Phobos and Deimos have been described as sons of the Greek god of war. Some scientists believe that the two moons are captured asteroids.

You board the landing module again for a quick trip to Phobos. At a distance of about 3,700 miles from the surface of Mars, it's the closer of the two moons. As you approach, you see that Phobos is dark and lumpy—somewhat like a potato. One crater, called Stickney, yawns five miles wide. It's about one-third the length of Phobos. This heavily cratered moon somehow survived a collision with an object that could have blown it to bits. After landing, you explore the surface carefully. If you bounce around too much, you could bound into space. Gravity on Phobos is extremely weak. If you weigh 100 pounds, a jump that would send you upward one foot on Earth could send you 1,000 feet upward on Phobos!

Like Earth's moon, Phobos always keeps the same face toward its planet. From Phobos, you have a clear view of a dust storm swirling across the Martian surface. But you don't have time to watch it, for you must return to *Odyssey* and prepare to lift off. You're on your way to the world of the outer planets.

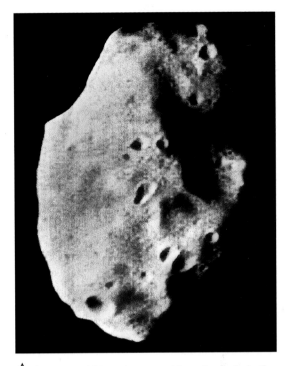

▲ *A meteoroid impact tore a king-size hole in the surface of Phobos. With its cratered, irregular shape, the moon looks a bit like a giant potato. Many scientists think Phobos, and Mars' other moon, Deimos, are captured asteroids.*

The Asteroid Belt: Space Debris

The asteroid belt is a wide area of rock-and-metal objects circling the sun between Mars and Jupiter. Most asteroids range in size from boulders to mountain-size chunks. Thousands measure more than half a mile across. Asteroids may be left over from the time when the planets formed. Some scientists believe that Jupiter's strong gravitational pull may have kept the rocks from forming a planet. Sometimes, when asteroids collide, pieces called meteoroids chip off. When a meteoroid enters Earth's atmosphere, it appears as a streak of light known as a meteor, or shooting star. If a meteoroid should reach Earth's surface, it's called a meteorite. Recovered meteorites contain iron, nickel, and rock. By studying meteorites, scientists hope to find clues to how the solar system formed.

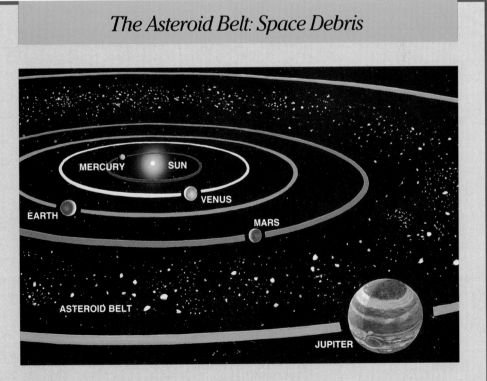

After a hike through a Martian canyon, young explorers welcome a ride back to their living quarters at a research base. Such a base does not exist now, of course; an artist created this view of one. But a research base will probably be built on Mars in the 21st century. Scientists and their families would live in underground complexes. They would grow their own food, distill oxygen and water from Martian soil, and collect power from the sun. Radio dishes would maintain contact with Earth and, free from most of Earth's radio noise, listen for signals from space.

4

The Outer Planets

"We have passed through the asteroid belt and are approaching the half-billion-mile marker in our tour," the captain announces. Glancing back, you notice that the sun seems much smaller. Because it is so far away, its energy is greatly weakened. The captain switches from solar power to nuclear power to run *Odyssey*'s electrical equipment. Coming up next in your journey: the five outer planets. Thick atmospheres blanket four of them. All together, the outer planets hold more than 50 moons in orbit. Jupiter, Saturn, and Uranus are circled by rings made up of countless small particles. Neptune may have partial rings. Saturn and its rings, in an image made with a radio telescope and painted false colors by a computer, glow like a neon sign (right). Pluto is truly the odd planet out. Small and solid, it's unlike the other outer planets. But before you puzzle over its mysteries, you'll call on the giants of the solar system.

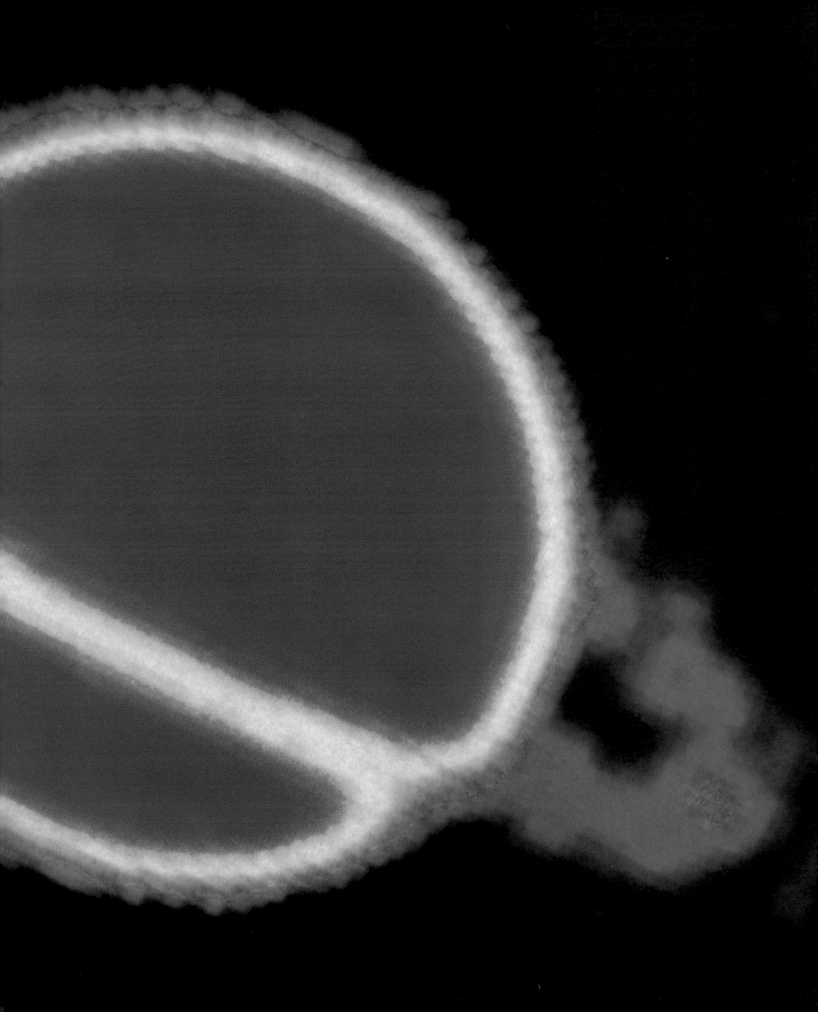

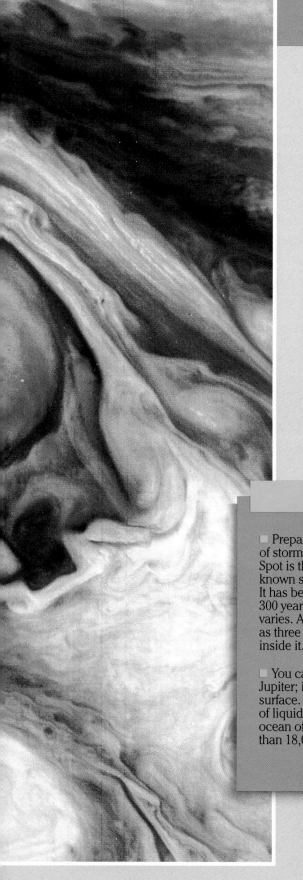

Jupiter

As *Odyssey* swings close to Jupiter (right), the largest planet in the solar system, you feel as if you were looking through a kaleidoscope. Everything seems to be in constant motion. Clouds swirl in dizzying combinations of patterns and colors. You see light and dark bands of clouds, and a large oval known as the Great Red Spot. It's the biggest of Jupiter's long-lasting storms. You look closely and see an orange moon to the right of the Great Red Spot.

You send out a remote-control probe to explore Jupiter's bands of clouds. The probe disappears into the clouds and sends back information. You discover that winds up to four times hurricane force drive the clouds. Lighter bands, called zones, move parallel to the planet's equator in one direction. Darker bands, called belts, move in the opposite direction. Jupiter rotates on its axis once about every ten hours. Such rapid rotation helps divide the clouds into these bands.

Reading data that the probe transmits to *Odyssey*, you learn that Jupiter's

Traveler's Bulletin

☐ Prepare to witness the king of storms. Jupiter's Great Red Spot is the longest-running known storm in the universe. It has been raging for at least 300 years. The storm's size varies. At its largest, as many as three Earths would fit inside it.

☐ You can't set foot on Jupiter; it has no solid surface. It does have a layer of liquid hydrogen. This ocean of hydrogen is hotter than 18,000°F.

☐ Jupiter's day is the shortest in the solar system. It lasts a few minutes less than 10 Earth hours.

☐ Jupiter is 2½ times the size of all the other planets combined. It would take 1,300 Earths to fill Jupiter.

☐ If you weigh 100 pounds on Earth, you'd weigh 254 pounds on Jupiter.

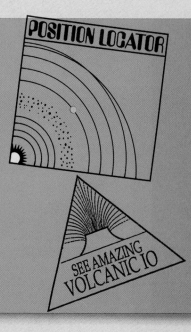

POSITION LOCATOR

SEE AMAZING VOLCANIC IO

◁ *Storm warning! In Jupiter's Great Red Spot, fierce winds create a storm of whirling clouds. A smaller storm shows up as a nearby oval. Scientists aren't sure why the Great Red Spot is red—a color enhanced by computer here.*

61

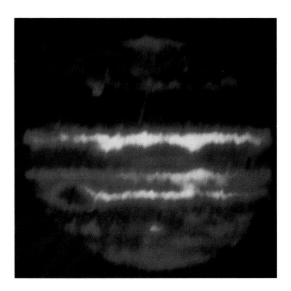

In this infrared image of Jupiter, bright areas indicate regions of high temperature. The hot spots show up through holes in the planet's cold cloud cover. Infrared measurements made from spacecraft confirmed an earlier conclusion of scientists: Jupiter gives off nearly twice as much energy as it receives from the sun.

coldest and highest clouds are red. The warmest and lowest clouds are blue. Other clouds are white and tan. What tints the clouds? Scientists aren't sure, but the colors may be caused by traces of phosphorus, sulfur, or even organic compounds.

As you direct the probe back to *Odyssey*, the planet expert explains that, beneath Jupiter's colorful clouds, increasing pressure causes hydrogen to change from a gas to a liquid. In fact, the planet's "surface" is a vast ocean of liquid hydrogen. Deep in this ocean, the liquid hydrogen acts like molten metal. As Jupiter spins, the metal flows, creating electric currents that generate a powerful magnetic field around the planet. The hydrogen ocean surrounds a rocky core. The core is about the same size as Earth, but contains much more material.

Jupiter grew so large, the planet expert says, because it formed in an area cold enough for water to freeze. Ice mixed with rocky particles to create the core. The planet's gravity swept up vast amounts of gases, especially hydrogen and helium. If Jupiter had been even more massive, the temperature and pressure at its core would have been high enough to generate nuclear reactions. Then Jupiter would have become a star, shining like the sun.

*A*lthough Jupiter falls short of shining on its own, its strong gravity affects other bodies around it. It tugs at other planets and changes the orbits of some comets. Its gravity may have prevented material in the asteroid belt from forming another planet.

Sixteen moons orbit Jupiter. The closest of the large moons,

Noisy Jupiter crackles and whistles

Jupiter is the noisiest planet. All planets send out radio waves, but Jupiter emits the strongest ones. In fact, except for the sun, Jupiter tunes in as the noisiest radio source in the solar system. You can "twirl the dial" on your radio telescope all you want, but Jupiter's radio waves will deliver no news, no talk shows, no music—just static and loud whistles.

When Io, a large moon of Jupiter, reaches a certain point in its orbit around the planet, it's as if an electrical switch were flipped on. The static and whistles grow stronger. As Io moves on, the electrical circuit breaks, and the static and whistles die down.

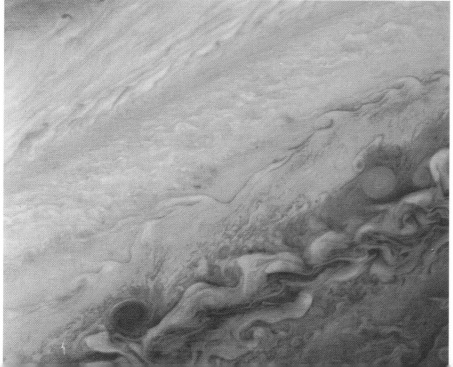

△ Sunlight reflects off tiny dust particles in Jupiter's ring system. Computer-added colors make it easier to see the three parts of the system. The main ring shows up as white. A region called the halo appears pink and yellow. The so-called gossamer ring, which appears red, circles Jupiter at a distance of about 130,000 miles from the center of the planet. Jupiter itself is not visible in this image.

◁ Carrying Jupiter's clouds around the planet, winds create a mix of cloud patterns. The straight, narrow orange band, upper left, marks an air current that zips along at more than 260 miles an hour. Wavy cloud patterns indicate winds that move more slowly.

63

The spacecraft Galileo, to be launched in 1989, focuses on Io, a moon of Jupiter. This painting shows a scene that won't happen until 1995. That's when Galileo is expected to reach Jupiter. The spacecraft will explore the planet and its Galilean moons. Here, sulfur compounds ejected from a volcano form wispy clouds on Io's horizon.

Io (EYE-oh), has no impact craters. In 1979, photographs made from Voyager spacecraft showed why. The photographs revealed *active* volcanoes, the only ones ever seen beyond Earth. Volcanic material had paved over craters. Instead of the molten rock that is ejected from Earth's volcanoes, however, liquid sulfur and sulfur dioxide probably shoot out of Io's volcanoes. In Io's weak gravity, volcanic material can spurt nearly 200 miles high, traveling as fast as 2,230 miles an hour. As it cools, it takes on a variety of colors: red, yellow, orange, black, white.

What might cause Io's volcanoes to erupt? Io lies within the gravitational fields of Jupiter and of two moons, Europa and Ganymede. Io is pulled first one way by Jupiter and then another by the moons. This makes Io move inward to the planet, and then outward. Io's changing distances from Jupiter cause the moon's surface to heave up and down as if it were an ocean tide. As a result of the movement, heat builds up inside Io. The volcanoes release the heat.

*R*adiation alert! The captain announces that it is dangerous to stay close to Jupiter and Io any longer because of deadly radiation. *Odyssey* pulls away and heads for a quick flyby of three other large moons of Jupiter: Europa, Ganymede, and Callisto.

Europa, which may be the smoothest object in the solar system, reminds you of a frozen snowball. A thin, smooth shell of ice covers the surface. Dark lines mark places where huge cracks may have split the surface long ago. The next moon, Ganymede, is the solar system's largest. It's about $1\frac{1}{2}$ times the size of Earth's moon. Ganymede's ice-and-rock surface bears impact craters and mountains. Finally, Callisto comes into view. Craters cover its icy surface. Rings of jumbled crust form bull's-eye patterns around areas where large objects hit Callisto billions of years ago.

With moons on your mind, you turn your attention to upcoming Saturn, the planet with more moons than any other.

▷ *Each of Jupiter's four largest moons is bigger than Pluto. Galileo Galilei, an Italian astronomer, discovered them in 1610. Astronomers today usually refer to them as the Galilean moons. Callisto, top, has the most crater-pocked surface. White areas in this photograph mark spots where objects hit the surface and exposed fresh ice. Ganymede, second from top, checks in as the largest moon in the solar system. It is even bigger than Mercury. A thin layer of ice may make Europa, third from top, the smoothest object in the solar system. More than 100 volcanoes dot the surface of Io, bottom. From top to bottom, the order of these pictures matches the order of each moon's distance from Jupiter: Callisto is farthest away and Io is closest. At least 12 smaller moons make up the rest of Jupiter's family.*

Fountains of sulfur light up the sky in this artist's view of Io. From a spot near the moon's south pole, you see Jupiter looming in the background. Io is the most volcanically active body in the solar system. Its volcanoes spurt liquid sulfur and sulfur dioxide at speeds of up to 2,230 miles an hour. Some volcanic material may coat particles in Jupiter's ring system, barely visible here.

Saturn

Giant Jupiter must have inspired you to think big, because looming ahead is something that looks like the biggest phonograph record, grooves and all, in existence. It's the ring system of Saturn (left). The grooves actually are countless trillions of particles gathered in ringlets. The ringlets make up Saturn's seven named rings. Only Saturn has such a complex system of rings. Ice makes the rings bright. The icy particles range from some that are microscopic in size to some that are as big as a house.

Where did the rings come from? Perhaps, according to *Odyssey*'s planet expert, the particles in the rings are left over from the collision of a moon and a comet. Perhaps they are pieces of a moon that orbited too close to the planet and was pulled apart by Saturn's gravity. Or perhaps the particles are pieces of a would-be moon that never formed. Although the rings extend outward about 260,000 miles from Saturn's cloud cover, they are relatively thin—less than 40 feet thick in some places.

Traveler's Bulletin

◻ To communicate by radio signals with someone on Earth, you'll need patience. It will take at least three hours for you to send the signals from Saturn to Earth and to receive a response.

◻ Until the discovery of Uranus in 1781, people thought Saturn marked the edge of the solar system. That's because Saturn is the most distant planet that can easily be seen from Earth without a telescope.

◻ From outside edge to opposite outside edge, the rings of Saturn stretch almost 600,000 miles.

◻ If you weigh 100 pounds on Earth, you'd weigh 108 pounds on Saturn.

◻ Like Earth, Saturn tilts on its axis. Like Earth, then, Saturn probably has seasons. But since Saturn takes almost 30 Earth years to circle the sun, each season on Saturn would last almost 30 times longer than it does on Earth.

POSITION LOCATOR

★ ADMIT ONE ★ MOON TOUR

LAUNCH TITAN PROBE

◁ *Computer-added colors help scientists see that particles of various sizes make up the rings of Saturn. In normal light, the rings appear as smooth bands (above) and the planet has the color of butterscotch pudding.*

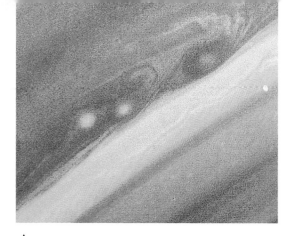

△ *A computer added colors to this image of clouds on Saturn. The colors show that cloud patterns on Saturn are similar to those on Jupiter. But winds around Saturn's equator are about four times as strong as winds around Jupiter.*

▽ *Scientists at the Jet Propulsion Laboratory, in California, study Voyager 1 images of Saturn. Two Voyager spacecraft were launched in 1977. They have sent back more information about Jupiter and Saturn than had been recorded since the invention of the telescope nearly 400 years ago.*

Compared with Jupiter, and with its own bright rings, Saturn itself looks dull. Its clouds lack the range of colors that you saw in Jupiter's clouds, perhaps because the circulation of Saturn's atmosphere mixes different clouds. Below Saturn's clouds, winds race about four times as fast as they do around Jupiter.

But Saturn and Jupiter have more in common than meets the eye. Both planets consist mainly of hydrogen; both have magnetic fields; and both have oval-shaped storm systems. Saturn is close to Jupiter in size, and has the second largest mass of the planets, with 95 times more material than Earth. Saturn's material is packed loosely, however. The planet is only 70 percent as dense as water. Because of its low density, Saturn would float in water!

Saturn has more moons than any other planet. You can count 17, but there may be even more. *Odyssey* heads for Titan, Saturn's largest moon and the solar system's second largest.

An orange smog hides Titan's surface. You ride a landing module through the atmosphere to find out what lies beneath it. Your instruments record that Titan's thick atmosphere, like Earth's, consists mostly of nitrogen. The instruments also detect methane, a poisonous gas. As you maneuver the module through Titan's

orange clouds, Saturn disappears and the sky grows darker. Flakes of methane snow fly around you. Jagged cliffs of frozen methane and seas containing some liquid methane come into view. Like water on Earth, methane on Titan can exist as a gas, a liquid, or a solid.

You decide to hover above Titan rather than risk landing. Pressure on the surface of this moon is about the same as it is on Earth, so you would face no danger of being crushed by the atmosphere. But the gooey, tarlike substance on the surface is not your idea of the perfect landing pad. The goo may be 300 feet thick in places.

Organic compounds that make up the goo are similar to those that make up familiar life-forms. But temperature sensors pick up a reading of –292°F. That's too cold for life to develop. Some scientists think that temperatures on Titan may once have been warmer, and that life-forms may have developed and later died out when temperatures dropped. If Titan ever was warm enough for the development of life, fossils could be buried in the goo or frozen in the methane ice. That discovery will have to await future explorers.

The landing module rises through the orange clouds. Saturn reappears. You board *Odyssey*. Another ringed world lies ahead. It's time to head for Uranus.

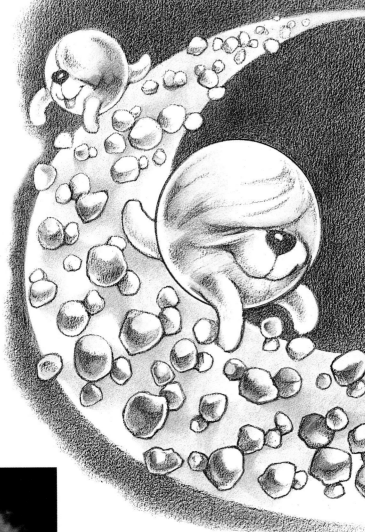

DIAMETER OF ENCELADUS: 311 MILES

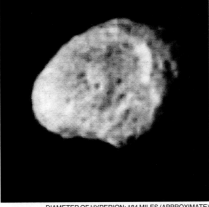

DIAMETER OF HYPERION: 184 MILES (APPROXIMATE)

Saturn has 17 known moons—more than any other planet. Most are icy spheres. Enceladus (above, left) is like a giant snowball. Some scientists think that liquid from inside the moon may occasionally escape through cracks in the surface and pave the moon with new ice. Hyperion (above, right) is also icy, but it looks more like a potato than a snowball. Objects that crashed into Hyperion broke off chunks of the moon. Titan (right) is one of the few moons in the solar system known to have an atmosphere. Organic compounds give Titan its orange color.

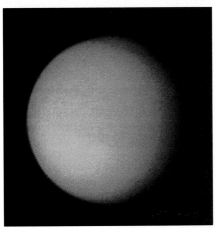

DIAMETER OF TITAN: 3,200 MILES

What keeps some of Saturn's rings from getting out of line?

Like sheepdogs, "shepherd moons" herd the particles in some of the rings. Voyager spacecraft discovered two tiny, irregularly shaped shepherd moons orbiting on either side of Saturn's "F" ring. The gravity of each of these shepherd moons holds the ring particles in place.

The outer moon orbits at a slightly slower speed than the ring particles. The inner moon moves slightly faster. When particles get close to the outer moon, its gravity slows them enough to send them falling toward Saturn. When particles approach the inner moon, its gravity speeds them up. Their increased energy sends them temporarily into a slightly wider orbit. Together, the two moons keep the "F" ring in place around Saturn.

Saturn looms beyond cratered plains on Rhea, the largest of its major inner moons. In this painting, sunlight reflected from Saturn brightens Rhea's surface. Saturn's rings appear thin because you are looking at their edges. The shadow of the rings forms a dark band across the planet. You can see the other four large inner moons in the distance. Like Rhea, they orbit outside the rings.

Uranus, Neptune, and Pluto

Full speed ahead! To reach Uranus, *Odyssey*'s captain accelerates to top speed: one-tenth the speed of light, or about 70 million miles an hour. Why so fast? You've got a long way to go! Uranus (right) is about $1\frac{1}{2}$ billion miles from the sun—19 times Earth's distance from the sun. As far away as Uranus is, it still marks only the midpoint of your planetary tour.

On the long journey to Uranus, you check *Odyssey*'s computer information bank. You learn that the upper atmospheres of Uranus and Neptune contain mostly hydrogen and helium. In addition, the two planets have large amounts of water, ammonia, and methane, which may be the result of collisions with comets. Uranus has rings; Neptune may have rings, too, but they don't appear to circle the entire planet.

Finally, Uranus comes into view. Methane clouds wrap the planet in a greenish blue envelope that hides any features in the atmosphere, such as

Traveler's Bulletin

□ Uranus and Neptune may contain diamonds! Great pressure and high temperatures near the cores may have freed carbon from methane and squeezed the carbon into diamonds.

□ Uranus and Neptune are greenish blue because the methane in their atmospheres absorbs red wavelengths in sunlight.

□ Like the other large outer planets, Uranus and Neptune are gas giants.

□ Colliding comets may have helped form Uranus and Neptune.

□ Temperatures around Uranus, Neptune, and Pluto probably stay colder than −350°F. If you exposed your bare hand while visiting one of these planets, it would be freeze-dried instantly.

□ If you weigh 100 pounds on Earth, you'd weigh 91 pounds on Uranus, 119 pounds on Neptune, and only about 8 pounds on Pluto!

◁ *Narrow rings circle Uranus. Most of them are only a few miles wide—much narrower than Saturn's rings. In this image, you can see a small section of the rings of Uranus. Computer-added colors make the dark rings visible.*

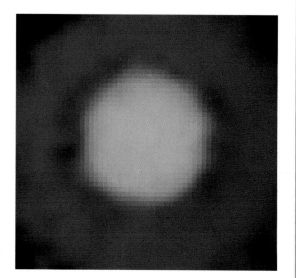

▽ *In an infrared view of Uranus, the rings appear blended together in a red halo around the planet. In this image, you look directly at one of the planet's poles and see the rings circling the equator. The image is fuzzy, partly because of disturbances in Earth's atmosphere.*

storms or bands of clouds. Since you can't detect any movement of features, it's hard to tell that Uranus is rotating.

You photograph the planet through filters. A computer enhances the images so that slight variations in the atmosphere show up. Now you can see that winds create bands of clouds around Uranus, as they do around Jupiter and Saturn. What lies below the clouds? No one knows, but *Odyssey*'s planet expert offers two theories. Perhaps the atmosphere thickens, changing to a watery slush near the planet's rocky core, or perhaps an ocean of superhot water and ammonia lies between the atmosphere and the core.

With a computer, you brighten images of the rings that are nearly invisible in your photographs. The rings are much narrower than the rings of Saturn. Most of the particles within the rings are as big as boulders. Nevertheless, the rings are hard to see because the particles are very dark.

Miranda is one of 15 moons that orbit Uranus and one of the oddest moons in the entire solar system. A flyby shows that grooves, canyons, and high cliffs mark Miranda's surface. Scientists say that many objects have hit Miranda, and that the moon may have shattered. The pieces were reassembled helter-skelter by gravity. Recent evidence from Voyager 2 suggests another possible explanation for the moon's appearance. Perhaps, during Miranda's formation, rocky material sank to the core and icy material rose to the surface, which froze before it had a chance to smooth out.

Leaving Uranus and Miranda, you set your sights on Neptune, the last of the gas giants, and on Triton. Of Neptune's two known moons, Triton is closer to the planet. Neptune appears to be much like Uranus. But Triton is in a class by itself. It is the only large moon that orbits its planet in a direction opposite that in which the planet

Uranus:
Down for the count

An unexpected meeting with an object the size of Earth may have knocked Uranus onto its side. Every other planet spins on its axis like a top, as Earth does. The axis of Uranus, however, runs nearly parallel to the planet's orbit, so Uranus appears to roll along part of its orbit like a ball. Scientists think Uranus may have received its knock-out punch early in its history. The rings, as well as the moons, may have resulted from the collision. Uranus' trip around the sun takes 84 Earth years. During the trip, one pole receives 42 years of daylight while the other has a 42-year night.

◁ Cliffs, grooves, and plains mark the patchwork surface of Miranda, smallest of Uranus' major moons. Scientists refer to the whitish V-shaped area, lower right, as "the chevron." The "V" and the grooved areas on either side of it developed more recently than the plains. Scientists combined several pictures of Miranda to make this one.

▽ An artist has painted Uranus as it might look from Miranda. In the foreground, ridges and grooves cut across the icy surface of Miranda like huge frozen tire tracks. Scientists think that thick, lumpy slush may have oozed out of cracks in the moon and frozen, forming the ridges.

True or false?
Pluto is the planet
farthest from the sun.

True. And false. Sometimes Pluto takes a vacation. During part of its orbit, Pluto swings inside Neptune's orbit and is then closer to the sun. Neptune remains the outermost planet as long as the switch in positions lasts—20 Earth years. Pluto is the only planet with an orbit that crosses inside another planet's orbit. But Pluto and Neptune will never collide. Pluto's orbit tilts so that it misses Neptune's orbit. Even when frigid Pluto moves almost 2 billion miles closer to the sun, its temperature rises only about 50 degrees, from −400°F to −350°F.

▼ *Voyager 2 made this portrait of Neptune and Triton. Of Neptune's two moons, Triton, which looks small here, is the larger. Methane colors Neptune greenish blue. Triton's shade of orange may come from organic compounds.*

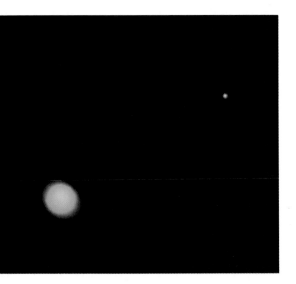

▶ *A painting of Triton shows a lake of liquid nitrogen and rocks coated with methane frost. Scientists don't know what the moon really looks like. It may have an atmosphere. Ice may cover its surface. Some of Triton's mysteries may be solved when Voyager 2 journeys past the moon in the summer of 1989.*

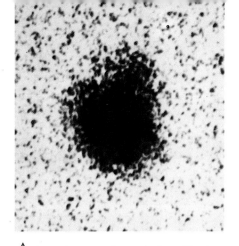

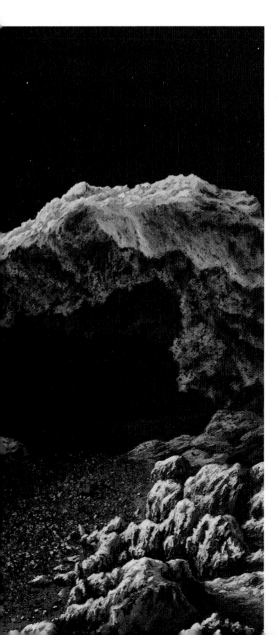

△ *In a photograph made from Earth and greatly magnified, Pluto appears to bulge at the top. In 1978, an astronomer noticed the bulge and determined it was actually a moon. The distance between Pluto and its moon, called Charon, is about 20 times less than the distance between Earth and its moon.*

spins. That makes Triton's orbit unstable. Eventually, the moon will spiral toward Neptune, break up, and perhaps form a ring.

Odyssey's planet expert explains that organic compounds probably color Triton a shade of orange. Parts of Triton's surface may be covered by nitrogen-methane ice or by shallow seas of liquid nitrogen. You would like to visit Triton, but the time has come to head for Pluto, the last known member of the sun's planetary family.

Pluto was discovered fairly recently, in 1930. The planet once was thought to be an icy moon of Neptune that somehow had been pulled into its own orbit around the sun. Then scientists discovered that Pluto contains more rock than ice, and has a moon of its own. Some experts now think that tiny Pluto, although called a planet, may actually be an asteroid of the outer solar system. A collision could have caused Pluto's moon to form and could have robbed the planet of much of its ice.

You aim *Odyssey*'s telescopes at Pluto and study the images they send to on-board monitors. You see ice, perhaps methane ice, on the planet's surface. You also see Pluto's moon, Charon. It orbits only about 12,000 miles away from Pluto, and its diameter is more than half that of the planet. Scientists consider Pluto and Charon—like Earth and its moon—a double planet.

Too soon, it seems, your space adventure is coming to an end. Before heading back to Earth, and home, you'll learn what lies in the darkness beyond Pluto.

The Mystery of Planet X

Something seems to be disturbing the orbits of Uranus and Neptune. Some astronomers think the cause may be Planet X, a tenth planet beyond Pluto. The mystery planet could take up to a thousand years to complete a single orbit around the sun. Astronomers calculate that Planet X, if it exists, is now in orbit somewhere within the region highlighted in red.

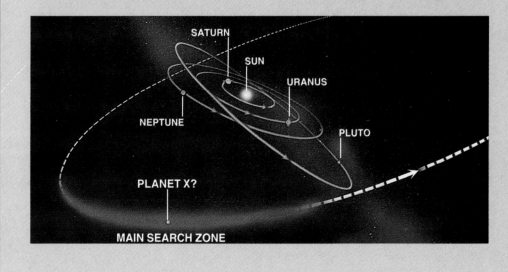

5

The Outer Limits

You have gone as far as *Odyssey* can take you. Before you head back to Earth, you want to learn about a region beyond the range of your spacecraft. Called the Oort cloud, it is believed to provide cold storage for trillions of comets. The Oort cloud is vast. It surrounds the sun and all its planets. Although no one has seen the Oort cloud, people have seen comets that may have come from there, like comet Bennett (right, in a false-color image).

You turn your attention to the tasks remaining on your journey. From *Odyssey*, you will launch a remote-control comet chaser to intercept and study a comet. You will also use a radio telescope to beam a message into space and to search the sky for radio signals. They may be coming from intelligent beings in other solar systems. If you pick up a signal from a civilization that is a thousand light-years away, that signal will be a thousand years old — the latest news from the ancient past.

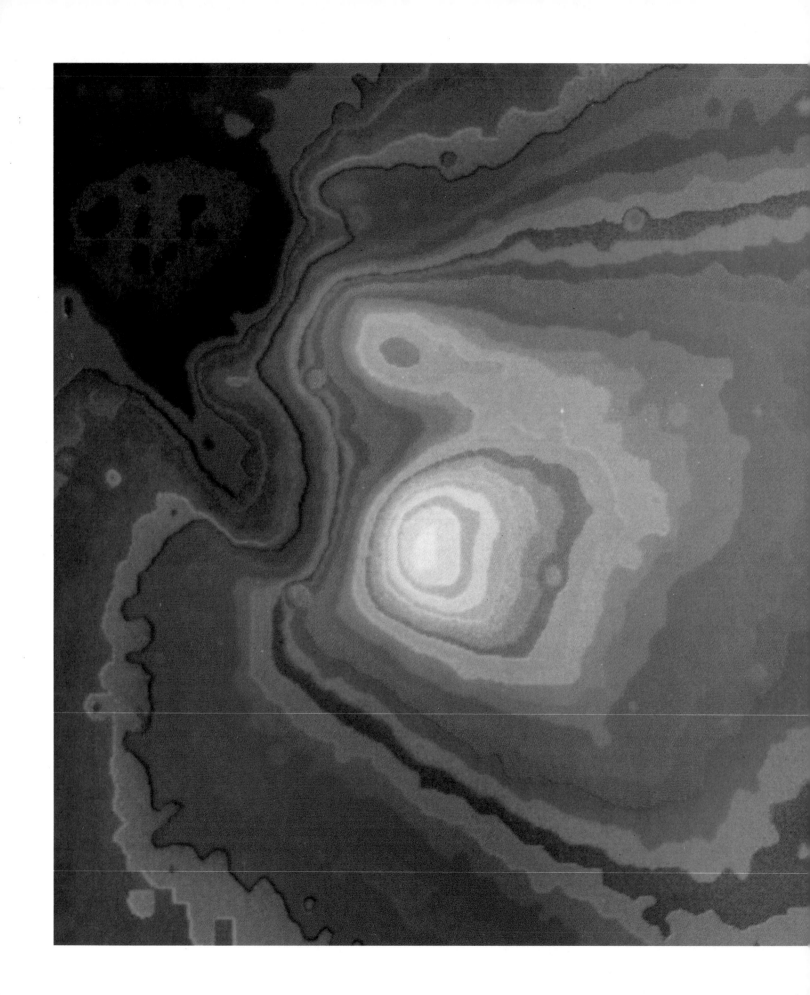

omets are messengers from the outer limits of the solar system. What messages do they bring? *Odyssey*'s comet expert says they may contain clues that would help tell us what materials existed when the solar system formed. Most comets in the Oort cloud are concentrated in an area 10,000 to 50,000 times farther from the sun than Earth is. For more than four billion years, these faraway comets have not been affected by the sun's heat.

The comet expert explains that the gravity of a passing star may scatter some comets in the Oort cloud and send them plunging toward the inner solar system. These comets—called long-period comets—take anywhere from 200 years to more than 4 million years to complete a single orbit. If such a comet is captured by the gravity of one of the giant outer planets, the comet's orbit may be shortened. Then the comet would become a short-period comet, requiring no more than 200 years to complete an orbit. Halley's

◀ *What looks like a colorful painting is an image of Halley's comet. Computer-added colors show levels of brightness. The dark area, upper left, is part of the nucleus. The white area is the brightest part of a jet of dust escaping from a crack in the nucleus.*

▶ *This dark, peanut-shaped object is a visible light image of the nucleus of Halley's comet. The images on these two pages were made by the Halley Multicolour Camera on board Giotto, a European Space Agency spacecraft.*

Traveler's Bulletin

■ Look carefully for hard-to-see comet nuclei. Along with some asteroids and the ring particles of Uranus, comet nuclei are among the darkest objects in the solar system.

■ Use your on-board radio telescope to search for signals from extraterrestrials. If you pick up a signal from a place thousands of light-years away, and if you send a response, your reply must also travel thousands of light-years before reaching its destination.

■ Only a comet with an orbit that passes near the sun develops a tail.

■ A comet's tail may easily stretch as far as the distance between Earth and Mars.

■ The man-made object that has traveled farthest in the solar system is Pioneer 10. Launched by the U. S. in 1972, this spacecraft has passed beyond Pluto's orbit.

■ An average of five to ten new comets are discovered every year. Amateur astronomers make most of the discoveries.

comet is the most famous short-period comet. It can be spotted from Earth every 76 years. Both long-period and short-period comets journey toward the inner solar system. Other comets may be hurled into interstellar space, out of reach of the sun's gravity.

You and your crew launch *Odyssey*'s comet chaser on a path that will intercept a comet. Any comet encountered here, in the frigid outer reaches of the solar system, will consist only of a nucleus—a small chunk of ice mixed with dust. Your comet expert explains that the nucleus will change as it passes through the asteroid belt and gets closer to the heat of the sun. Some of the ice will change to gas. Cracks will open in the surface of the nucleus. Gas and dust released through the cracks will form a cloud, called a coma, around the nucleus. A tail will stream away from the coma.

Usually a comet's tail consists of two parts: a straight gas tail and a curved dust tail. By the time a comet nears Earth's orbit, the coma could be as big as Jupiter, and the tail could stretch the distance from Earth to Mars! As a comet swings past the sun and heads out of the inner solar system, its tail is ahead of it rather than behind. The solar wind and the pressure of radiation from the sun keep comet tails pointing away from the sun.

*I*n 1908, in the Tunguska River valley of Siberia, in the Soviet Union, an explosion as powerful as an atomic bomb flattened a forest almost as big as Rhode Island. Despite this massive damage, no crater scarred the ground. Some scientists think that the mysterious explosion was caused by a comet that entered Earth's atmosphere and blew up before it reached the ground. Your comet expert

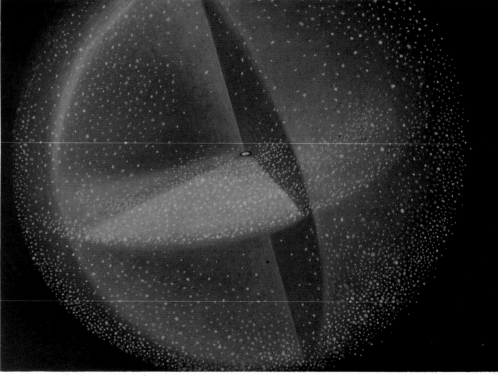

▶ *Some scientists believe comets come from a disk-shaped ring that extends across the solar system far beyond Pluto's orbit. The ring contains about five trillion comets. It gradually fans out to form a sphere around the solar system. This sphere may contain a trillion more comets. The ring and sphere together are known as the Oort cloud. In this diagram, the white dot at the center represents the sun and its entire family of planets. Comets have existed, scientists believe, since the solar system developed. When Uranus and Neptune formed, their gravity may have caused some comets to collide with the inner planets. Other comets may have been thrown into the outer regions of the solar system, where they collected, forming the Oort cloud.*

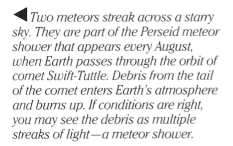

◀ *Two meteors streak across a starry sky. They are part of the Perseid meteor shower that appears every August, when Earth passes through the orbit of comet Swift-Tuttle. Debris from the tail of the comet enters Earth's atmosphere and burns up. If conditions are right, you may see the debris as multiple streaks of light—a meteor shower.*

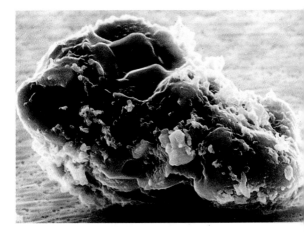

▲ *It looks huge, but it's a tiny piece of dust magnified 15,000 times. Scientists think it may once have been part of a comet's nucleus. Comet dust is harmless. It drifts constantly through the air around you.*

Away from home: Comets on the move

Scientists have different theories about why comets leave the cold storage of the Oort cloud. The gravity of a passing star (right) may send a comet out of the cloud toward the inner solar system. The gravity of huge clouds of hydrogen called giant molecular clouds may strip millions of comets from the Oort cloud. Or the tidal force of the galaxy may tug comets out of the Oort cloud.

Once a comet enters the inner solar system, it may be flung by Jupiter's gravity into a long, cigar-shaped orbit . . . or it may crash into the sun, into a moon, or into a planet. As many as five million comets may have hit Earth during its first billion years, according to some comet experts.

believes that, once every 300 to 500 million years, a shower of comets may collide with Earth. Could previous collisions have created dust clouds that blocked out sunlight and led to the extinction of dinosaurs? Could encounters with Earth's atmosphere have changed comet ice into rain—enough to form Earth's early oceans? Could comets that collided with Earth have brought with them some of the building blocks of life? Some scientists believe the answer to each of these questions is "yes," but no one knows for sure.

As you discuss these fascinating possibilities with your comet expert, you are interrupted by an announcement: "Begin preparations for the trip back to Earth." You are sorry your journey will soon be ending, but excited about returning home.

You know reporters will be at the landing site to meet you. You wish you could bring them messages from other life-forms. *Odyssey*'s specialist in the search for extraterrestrial intelligence, or SETI, says there's a good chance that such life-forms exist. There might be thousands of civilizations on thousands of planets in the Milky Way Galaxy alone. You won't be able to search for them on this trip, however. It would take too long, and you don't have enough fuel.

The SETI expert tells you that some scientists believe the first extraterrestrial contact, if it takes place, will come through radio signals, which travel at the speed of light. Using radio telescopes, scientists scan the skies for unusual signals. They pay close attention

▲ *In 1974, a message—shown here in a visual display—was beamed to a star cluster 24,000 light-years away. The red stick figure represents a human being and the yellow markings stand for the solar system. The blue spirals represent DNA, the basic molecule of life on Earth.*

▶ *A radio telescope at Harvard, Massachusetts, searches the sky for radio signals from civilizations in space.*

to certain radio bands that intelligent beings might use to transmit messages. No one has received a message yet, but you might be the lucky one. You check out the supercomputer signal analyzer connected to *Odyssey*'s radio telescope. On the monitor, you see a graph showing a strong signal. Could this be *it*, the first signal from another civilization that scientists have been searching for? Your excitement mounts, but the SETI expert determines that the graph shows a signal that has come from a radio broadcast on Earth.

You decide to compose your own message to any extraterrestrials that might be out there. In computer code, you state your name and describe Earth's location in the galaxy and solar system. You use a phased-array antenna to beam the message to a thousand sunlike stars in the galaxy—those nearest Earth. Such stars might have planets like the sun's. You know that the signals, as they travel through space, could be received in a hundred years or less. You try to imagine what kinds of life-forms might receive them.

These thoughts make you realize how much you miss the most familiar forms of life—your family and friends. You'll see them all soon. Your voyage to the other apparently lifeless planets has made you appreciate how precious life on Earth is. You make up your mind that, as you continue to study the solar system, you will work hard to protect Earth's environment.

Now make yourself comfortable. Your return trip has begun!

▼ *Beta Pictoris, a star roughly twice the size of the sun, shines about 50 light-years away from our solar system. Scientists think the thin disk of dust visible around the star in this telescope image may be evidence that planets and comets are developing in another solar system.*

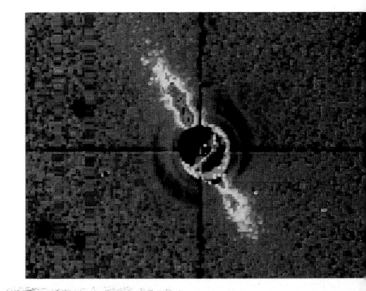

Does rock and roll have a galaxy of fans?

Rock and roll star Elvis Presley first appeared on national TV in 1955. By 1990, radio waves carrying the Elvis broadcast will be 35 light-years (more than 200 trillion miles) from Earth. That's because such waves travel at the speed of light. If there are life-forms on planets around the nearby star Vega, in the Milky Way, they might pick up signals from the broadcast. The galaxy is about 100,000 light-years wide. Tens of thousands of years will pass before the waves from Elvis' performance travel out of the galaxy.

Most scientists who hope to make contact with extraterrestrial life think the best way to do so is to search for radio signals from space. For about 30 years, they have been trying to pick up any unusual repeating signals—so far without success. Soon astronomers hope to use their radio telescopes, along with new computers, in the biggest search yet.

Fire and ice—volcanoes and glaciers— characterize an artist's view of an imaginary planet. Many forms of intelligent life might develop on a planet where areas are isolated by mountains or oceans. Here the artist shows an insect-like creature and a lizard-like creature trading tools for furs. While they do business, another creature bathes in springs heated by volcanic activity.

Glossary

Asteroid: a rock-and-metal object that orbits the sun. Some are as small as a boulder; some are hundreds of miles across. Most orbit between Mars and Jupiter in a region called the **asteroid belt**. Asteroids are sometimes referred to as minor planets.

Atmosphere: the gases that surround a planet, a comet, or sometimes a moon; also, the outer layers of a star.

Axis: an imaginary line that runs pole to pole through a planet or other body. The body rotates, or turns, around the line.

Chromosphere: the layer of the sun's atmosphere just above the photosphere, or surface layer of gases. The term "chromosphere" means "color sphere," and the chromosphere is so named because the hydrogen it contains gives off red light.

Comet: a chunk of ice mixed with dust that orbits the sun. Some comets are miles across. When a comet passes near the sun, some of its ice changes to gas, creating a **coma**—a cloud of dust and gas, and a **tail**—a stream of dust and gas that always points away from the sun. Trillions of comets are thought to exist in a region that stretches far beyond Pluto, known as the Oort cloud.

Corona: the outermost layer of the sun's atmosphere. It begins above the chromosphere and extends for millions of miles.

Coronal hole: a region where the corona seems to be absent. Solar wind escapes through coronal holes.

Density: a measure of how tightly the material of a substance or object is packed into a given space.

Eclipse: total or partial blocking of light from a body in space caused by another body passing in front of it. In a solar eclipse, Earth's moon passes between Earth and the sun, temporarily blocking out sunlight to Earth.

Galaxy: a system of stars—sometimes billions of them—and other matter, such as nebulae, held together by gravity.

Gravity: the force of a planet, a moon, or other object that pulls mass toward its center.

Greenhouse effect: the warming of a planet's or moon's lower atmosphere and surface that occurs when energy from the sun is trapped by certain gases in the body's atmosphere.

Impact crater: a depression on a body in the solar system made by a collision with a meteoroid, comet, or asteroid.

Interstellar space: the vast reaches of space between stars.

Light-year: the distance light travels through space in one Earth year—about six trillion (6,000,000,000,000) miles.

Magnetic field: the region of space around a body in which that body exerts magnetic force. Earth's magnetic field shields the planet by repelling solar wind.

Mare (MAHR-ay): a large, relatively smooth, dark area on the surface of a planet or moon, made of hardened lava. (Plural: **maria**, pronounced MAHR-ee-uh)

Mass: the amount of matter, or material, that an object has.

Meteoroid: a solid body smaller than an asteroid that orbits the sun. When it passes through Earth's atmosphere, the streak of light created is called a **meteor**. If a meteoroid hits Earth, it is called a **meteorite**.

Moon: a natural satellite orbiting a planet.

Nebula: a cloud of gas and dust in space, appearing as either a glowing or dark region. (Plural: **nebulae**)

Oort cloud: a region at the outer limits of our solar system that is believed to contain trillions of comets.

Orbit: the path that a body in space takes around another body in space.

Ozone layer: a layer of ozone molecules—each composed of three oxygen atoms—in Earth's atmosphere. The layer absorbs most of the sun's ultraviolet radiation, protecting life on Earth.

Photosphere: the visible layer of gases that make up what is commonly thought of as the sun's surface.

Planet: a body in space larger than an asteroid that is held in orbit around a star by the star's gravity. A planet is bright because it reflects the light of the star it orbits.

Regolith: a layer of dust and rock fragments on the surface of a planet or other body in space that builds up when meteoroids, asteroids, and comets strike the body.

Revolution: the motion of a planet or other object—a moon, asteroid, or comet—in its orbit. One complete revolution of a body equals one year for that body.

Rotation: the turning of a body around its axis. One complete turn equals one day for that body.

Scarp: a type of cliff on a planet or moon. On Mercury, scarps can be up to two miles high.

Solar system: a term commonly used to describe our sun and the objects that revolve around it. These include the nine known planets, many moons, thousands of asteroids, billions of meteoroids, and trillions of comets. Other solar systems may exist or may be forming.

Solar wind: electrically charged particles that escape the sun, mostly through coronal holes, and flow into the solar system.

Star: a hot, glowing sphere of gas that radiates, or used to radiate, energy from nuclear reactions in its core.

Sunspots: highly magnetic areas in the sun's photosphere that appear dark because they are cooler than the gases surrounding them.

Transit: in the solar system, the passage of a small body in front of a larger one. This differs from an eclipse in that very little light from the larger body is blocked. For instance, from Earth, Venus and Mercury can sometimes be seen in transit across the sun.

Coming Attractions

Exploring Your Universe: *This list includes a few of the many space explorations planned by NASA (National Aeronautics and Space Administration) into 1996. The list is based on information available as of February 1989.*

1989 *April:* Launch of Magellan from the shuttle *Atlantis* to study Venus. Magellan is expected to reach Venus in August 1990.

July: Launch of COBE (Cosmic Background Explorer) from a Delta rocket to study cosmic radiation.

August: Closest approach of Voyager 2 (launched in 1977) to Neptune is expected on August 24; first spacecraft to fly by Jupiter, Saturn, Uranus, and Neptune.

October: Launch of Galileo from the shuttle *Atlantis* to study Jupiter and four of its moons. Galileo is expected to reach Jupiter in late 1995.

December: Launch of Hubble Space Telescope from the shuttle *Discovery* to study the planets, stars, galaxies, and the evolution of the universe.

1990 *February:* Launch of ROSAT (Roentgen Satellite) from a Delta rocket to study X-ray emissions from objects in space.

April: Launch of GRO (Gamma Ray Observatory) from the shuttle *Discovery* to study gamma-ray emissions from objects in space.

October: Launch of Ulysses from the shuttle *Atlantis* to study the sun. Ulysses is expected to near the sun in May 1994.

1991 *August:* Launch of EUVE (Extreme Ultraviolet Explorer) from a Delta rocket to study some stars, interstellar space.

1992 *September:* Launch of Mars Observer from a Titan III rocket to study the climate and mineral makeup of Mars.

1995 (Specific dates not determined)
Launch of AXAF (Advanced X-ray Astronomy Facility) to study subjects such as black holes, galaxies, and quasars.

Launch of CRAF (Comet Rendezvous Asteroid Flyby) to study comets and the asteroid belt. (Project status: proposed.)

Construction start-up for the space station Freedom. It will be ready for permanent habitation by 1996; finished by 1998.

1996 *Launch* of Cassini for study of Saturn and its moon Titan. (Project status: proposed)

Watching the Sky: *In the list below are some of the many natural events that will occur from 1989 through 1995. Depending on your location, you may see some simply by looking at the sky in the right place at the right time. For others, you will need a telescope. A sky chart will help you find them. An observatory, planetarium, or science museum may have more information on the events. (Warning: Never look directly at the sun.)*

1989 *All year, into 1990:* Sunspot activity peaks; this occurs at 11-year intervals. In far north, see brilliant auroras.

February–November: Gathering of Saturn, Uranus, and Neptune; this won't occur again for 180 years. With a sky chart and binoculars or a telescope, locate bright Saturn. Uranus is to its west; Neptune is to its north.

March 10–11: Gathering of Mars, Jupiter, and the Pleiades star cluster. Look high, west-southwest at dusk.

Early May: Eta Aquarid meteor shower, best seen from midnight to dawn. Shower is early May every year. It originates from Halley's comet.

August 16: Total lunar eclipse, visible from most of North America.

Mid-August: Perseid meteor shower, best seen from midnight to dawn. Shower is mid-August every year.

Early September: Pluto's closest approach to the sun; occurs every 248 years.

October 21: Orionid meteor shower best seen from midnight to dawn. Shower is this time every year. It originates from Halley's comet.

Mid-December: Geminid meteor shower best seen from midnight to dawn. Shower is mid-December every year.

December 27: Jupiter at its brightest for the year, visible all night. Look low, east-northeast at dusk.

1990 *May 7:* Closest approach of Pluto to Earth; occurs every 248 years.

July 21: Partial solar eclipse, seen from Hawaii and northwestern North America.

August 12, 13: Gathering of Venus and Jupiter in east morning sky.

Late November: Mars at its closest approach to Earth (48 million miles) and at its brightest for this year, visible all night. Look low, east-northeast at dusk. This double event occurs about every 2 years.

1991 *June:* Gathering of Venus, Mars, and Jupiter. Look west at dusk. On June 15, Earth's crescent moon joins these

three planets. On June 17, the planets form a tiny, glittering triangle.

July 11: Total solar eclipse, visible from Hawaii and from Mexico through South America. Visible as a partial eclipse from anyplace in North America except extreme east and north.

July 14: Gathering of Mercury and Jupiter. Look low, west-northwest at dusk. For a few evenings, Mercury, Venus, Mars, Jupiter, and Saturn are visible.

October 16: Gathering of Venus and Jupiter. Look high, east-southeast at dawn.

1992 *January 4:* Annular, or ring, solar eclipse, visible from the coast of southern California. Visible as partial eclipse from western U.S. and Canada.

February 28–29: Gathering of Venus, Mars, and Saturn. Look east-southeast at dawn.

June 14–15: Partial lunar eclipse, visible from most of North America.

December 9: Total lunar eclipse, seen from most of North America but far west.

1993 *All year:* Uranus overtakes Neptune. This event occurs about every 170 years. From Earth, the planets appear to pass each other three times—an event called a "triple conjunction."

May 21: Partial solar eclipse, visible from most of northern North America.

June 4: Total lunar eclipse, visible from Hawaii, southwestern Alaska, and the coast of California.

November 6: Mercury transits the sun; not visible from North America.

November 28-29: Total lunar eclipse, visible from most of North America.

1994 *May 10:* Annular solar eclipse. Visible as partial eclipse from anyplace in North America. In a path from New Mexico to New England, it is visible as a full annular eclipse.

Early June: Venus attains its highest position this year in the evening sky. In December, it will attain its highest position in the morning sky.

September 1: Saturn visible all night. Look low, east-southeast at dusk.

1995 *May 21–August 11:* Saturn's rings are edgewise to Earth, so are not visible—a rare occurrence.

June 1: Jupiter at its brightest for this year, visible all night.

November 15-22: Gathering of Venus, Mars, and Jupiter. Look very low, southwest at dusk.

Index

Bold type indicates illustrations;
regular type refers to text.

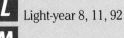
Two astronauts leave their spacecraft to explore Phobos, a Martian moon. One astronaut prepares to set foot on the moon; the other is beginning the descent. Scientists may someday build a base on Phobos. It could serve as a stopover on the way to Mars, shown looming in the background of this painting. The moon itself may contain water, carbon, nitrogen, and oxygen, and might provide resources for missions to Mars.

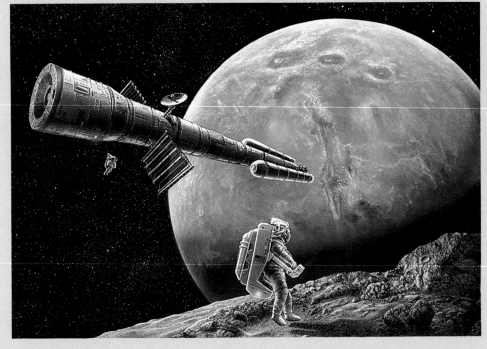

Additional Reading

Readers may want to check the *National Geographic Index* in a school or public library for related articles and to refer to the books, periodicals, and sky charts below. ("A" indicates material at the adult level.)

Periodicals and Sky Charts: *Astronomy,* Kalmbach Publishing Company (A). *Odyssey,* AstroMedia Corporation. *Sky Calendar,* Abrams Planetarium, Michigan State University. *Sky & Telescope,* Sky Publishing Corporation (A). *Star Date,* McDonald Observatory, The University of Texas (A).

General Reading: Ardley, Neil, *The Inner Planets,* and *The Outer Planets,* both Schoolhouse, 1988. Atkinson, Stuart, *Journey into Space,* Viking Penguin, 1988. Brandt, John C., and Stephen P. Maran, *New Horizons in Astronomy,* W.H. Freeman, 1979 (A). Branley, Franklyn M., *Saturn: The Spectacular Planet,* 1987, and *What the Moon is Like,* 1986, both Harper & Row Junior Books. Couper, Heather, and Nigel Henbest, *The Sun,* Franklin Watts, 1987. Hatchett, Clint, *The Glow-in-the-Dark Night Sky Book,* Random House, 1988. Humberstone, Eliot, *Finding Out About Things Outdoors,* EDC Publishing, 1981. Krupp, E.C., *The Comet and You,* Macmillan, 1985. McAleer, Neil, *The Omni Space Almanac,* Pharos Books, 1987. Miller, Ron, and William K. Hartmann, *The Grand Tour: A Traveler's Guide to the Solar System,* Workman Publishing Company, Inc., 1981. Moore, Patrick, *Guinness Book of Astronomy Facts and Feats,* Guinness Superlatives, Limited, 1988 (A). Myring, Lynn, *Finding Out About Rockets and Spaceflight,* EDC Publishing, 1982. Myring, Lynn, and Sheila Snowden, *Finding Out About Sun, Moon, and Planets,* EDC Publishing, 1982. Oberg, James E., and Alcestis R., *Pioneering Space: Living on the Next Frontier,* McGraw-Hill, 1986. Ottewell, Guy, *The Astronomical Companion,* Department of Physics, Furman University, 1979 (A). Pasachoff, Jay, *Peterson First Guide to Astronomy,* Houghton Mifflin, 1988 (A). Petty, Kate, *The Sun,* Franklin Watts, 1985. Ride, Sally, with Susan Okie, *To Space & Back,* Lothrop, Lee & Shepard Books, 1986. Snowden, Sheila, *The Young Astronomer,* EDC Publishing, 1983. Whitney, Charles, *Whitney's Star Finder,* Alfred Knopf, 1985 (A). Williams, Geoffrey T., and Dennis F. Regan, *Adventures in the Solar System: Planetron and Me,* Price/Stern/Sloan, 1986.

Science-Fiction Books: Asimov, Isaac, Martin Greenberg, and Charles G. Waugh (editors), *Young Star Travelers,* Harper & Row Junior Books, 1986. Bradbury, Ray, *The Martian Chronicles,* Doubleday, 1958. Lawrence, Louise, *Calling B for Butterfly,* Harper & Row Junior Books, 1982. Paton Walsh, Jill, *The Green Book,* Farrar, Straus, Giroux, 1982. Pinkwater, Daniel, *Fat Men From Space,* Dell, 1980. Sleator, William, *Interstellar Pig,* Bantam, 1986. Slote, Alfred, *My Trip to Alpha I,* Avon, 1985. Wells, H.G., *The War of the Worlds,* Putnam Publishing Group, (reprint) 1978.

By the National Geographic Society: *The Heavens* (map), 1982. *On the Brink of Tomorrow: Frontiers of Science,* 1982 (A). *Our Universe,* 1986. *Science: It's Changing Your World,* 1985. *Solar System/Saturn* (map), 1981. "Star Watching" (sky chart), *WORLD,* December 1979.

CONSULTANTS

Stephen P. Maran, Ph.D., Senior Staff Scientist,
NASA/Goddard Space Flight Center, *Chief Consultant*
Lynda Bush, Ph.D., *Reading Consultant*
Nicholas J. Long, Ph.D., *Consulting Psychologist*

The Special Publications and School Services Division is grateful to the individuals and institutions named or quoted within the text and to those cited here for their generous assistance:
American Association for the Advancement of Science; Paula Cleggett-Haleim, William L. Piotrowski, Geoffrey Vincent, NASA; Raymon G. Davie, Cooperstown, New York; Billie Deason, Mike Gentry, NASA/Johnson Space Center; Debra Meloy Elmegreen, Vassar College Observatory; Candice J. Hansen, Jurrie J. van der Woude, Paul R. Weissman, Jet Propulsion Laboratory; Robert S. Harrington, Paul M. Janiczek, U. S. Naval Observatory; William K. Hartmann, Planetary Science Institute; Thomas E. Holzer, Nita Razo, National Center for Atmospheric Research/NSF; Paul Horowitz, Harvard University; William B. Hubbard, Lunar and Planetary Laboratory, University of Arizona; Joel S. Levine, NASA/Langley Research Center; Christopher P. McKay, NASA/Ames Research Center; Frank H. Oram, World Population Society; Lawrence R. Pettinger, U.S. Geological Survey; Andrew Pogan, Montgomery County Schools, Maryland; Michael L. Rodemeyer, Jr., Glen Echo, Maryland; Lee Sentell, United States Space Camp; Steven Smith, Arlington Planetarium; Robert C. Victor, Abrams Planetarium, Michigan State University; Richard W. Vorder Bruegge, Brown University.

ILLUSTRATIONS CREDITS

Cover: Don Dixon. **Title Page:** Patrick Rawlings, Mark Dowman, and John Lowery/ Eagle Aerospace, Inc. **Introduction and Table of Contents:** NASA/Johnson Space Center (2 top); Kazuaki Iwasaki/The Stock Market (2 bottom); courtesy Harvard College Observatory (3 top); Margo H. Edwards, Raymond E. Arvidson, James R. Heirtzler (3 left); NASA (3 right). © 1988 Roger Ressmeyer/Starlight (3 bottom). **Chapter 1:** © 1980 Royal Observatory, Edinburgh (4-5); Ron Miller (6-7, 8-9 top); Akira Fujii (8-9 bottom); Richard Paresi/Bill Burrows & Associates (9 bottom right); © The Dille Family Trust (10 top left); Henry Burroughs/Associated Press (10 bottom left); NASA/Johnson Space Center (10-11); © Randa Bishop (11 right); Don Dixon (12-13). **Chapter 2:** National Center for Atmospheric Research/National Science Foundation (14-15); NASA/Johnson Space Center (16-17 both); Marvin J. Fryer (18 top); David R. Austen (18 bottom left); NASA/Marshall Space Flight Center (18-19 center); Akira Fujii (18-19 bottom); Big Bear Solar Observatory, California Institute of Technology (19 top); Project Stratoscope of Princeton University (19 bottom right); Solar Physics Group, American Science and Engineering and NASA (20 top); Richard Paresi/Bill Burrows & Associates (20 bottom); Richard A. Cooke III (21); Davis Meltzer (22-23). **Chapter 3:** NASA/Johnson Space Center (24-25, 39 top, 47 top); NASA/Jet Propulsion Laboratory (26-27 both, 51 top, 52-53, 53 both, 55 top); © Fred Espenak, 1989 (28 top); Richard Paresi/Bill Burrows & Associates (28 bottom, 34 left, 40 bottom right, 45 bottom, 52 bottom); NASA (29 both, 35 center and bottom); Don Dixon (30-31, 36-37, 46); courtesy of D. B. Campbell, Cornell University (32-33); NASA/Ames Research Center (33 top); Dennis DiCicco/*Sky & Telescope Magazine* (34 right); © Anglo-Australian Telescope Board, 1983 (35 top); courtesy of Environmental Research Institute of Michigan, Ann Arbor, Michigan (38-39); Harald Sund/The Image Bank (40 left); David Alan Harvey (40-41 top); Gerald Cubitt (41 right); © John H. Meehan/Science Source/Photo Researchers Inc. (42); Earth Scenes/OSF–Michael Fogden (43 top); Sally J. Bensusen (43 bottom, 55 bottom); Patricia Lanza (44 top); David Alan Brownell (44 bottom); Akira Fujii (45 top); NASA, David S. McKay and Uel S. Clanton (47 center); Dr. A. E. Bence/State University of New York in Stony Brook (47 bottom); Paul DiMare (48-49, 56-57); U.S. Geological Survey, Flagstaff, Arizona (50-51); © Michael Carroll (54). **Chapter 4:** Imke de Pater and John R. Dickel, using the VLA of the NRAO operated by AUI under contract with the NSF (58-59); NASA/Jet Propulsion Laboratory (60-61, 62 top, 63 bottom, 65 all, 68-69 both, 70 top, 71 center and bottom, 74-75 both, 77 top, 78 left); Richard Paresi/ Bill Burrows & Associates (62 bottom, 71 top, 76 bottom, 78 top); Mark R. Showalter and Joseph A. Burns/Cornell University (63 top); Kazuaki Iwasaki/The Stock Market (64, 66-67, 72-73); Douglas Kirkland/Contact Press (70 bottom); © Anglo-Australian Telescope Board, 1983 (76 bottom); Don Dixon (77 bottom, 80-81); © Marilynn Flynn (78-79); James W. Christy/Official U. S. Naval Observatory Photograph (79 top); Sally J. Bensusen (79 right). **Chapter 5:** © Fred Espenak, 1989 (82-83); © 1986 Max-Planck-Institut für Aeronomie, courtesy Dr. H. U. Keller (84-85 both); Akira Fujii (86-87); Davis Meltzer (86 bottom); NASA (87 top right); Richard Paresi/Bill Burrows & Associates (87 bottom, 89 bottom); National Astronomy and Ionosphere Center, operated by Cornell University under a management agreement with the National Science Foundation (88 left); Paul Horowitz (88 right); R. J. Terrile and B. A. Smith/Las Campanas Observatory (89 top); Thomas O. Miller (90-91); Don Dixon (94).

Library of Congress CIP Data

Rathbun, Elizabeth
  Exploring your solar system
  (Books for world explorers)
  Bibliography: p.
  Includes index.
  Summary: Presents a guided tour of the nine planets within the solar system. Also discusses the Milky Way Galaxy, comets, and the search for extraterrestrial intelligence.
  1. Solar system—Juvenile literature. 2. Outer space—Exploration—Juvenile literature.
  [1. Solar system. 2. Outer space] I. Title. II. Series.
  QB501.3.R38 1989   523.2   89-3138
  ISBN 0–87044–703–3 (regular edition)   ISBN 0–87044–708–4 (library edition)

Exploring Your
SOLAR SYSTEM

PUBLISHED BY
THE NATIONAL GEOGRAPHIC SOCIETY
WASHINGTON, D. C.

Gilbert M. Grosvenor, *President and Chairman of the Board*
Melvin M. Payne, Thomas W. McKnew, *Chairmen Emeritus*
Owen R. Anderson, *Executive Vice President*
Robert L. Breeden, *Senior Vice President,*
Publications and Educational Media

PREPARED BY THE SPECIAL PUBLICATIONS
AND SCHOOL SERVICES DIVISION
Donald J. Crump, *Director*
Philip B. Silcott, *Associate Director*
Bonnie S. Lawrence, *Assistant Director*

BOOKS FOR WORLD EXPLORERS
Pat Robbins, *Editor*
Ralph Gray, *Editor Emeritus*
Ursula Perrin Vosseler, *Art Director*
Margaret McKelway, *Associate Editor*
Larry Nighswander, *Illustrations Editor*

STAFF FOR
EXPLORING YOUR SOLAR SYSTEM
Margaret McKelway, Susan Mondshein Tejada
Managing Editors
Alison Wilbur Eskildsen, *Illustrations Editor*
Dorrit Green, *Art Director*
Lori Elizabeth Davie, Suzanne Nave Patrick, *Researchers*
Ross Bankson, M. Barbara Brownell, *Contributing Editors*
Barbara L. Bricks, *Contributing Researcher*
Kathryn N. Adams, Sandra F. Lotterman,
Nancy J. White, *Editorial Assistants*
Janet A. Dustin, Jennie H. Proctor, *Illustrations Assistants*

ENGRAVING, PRINTING, AND PRODUCT MANUFACTURE: George V. White, *Director*, and Vincent P. Ryan, *Manager*, Manufacturing and Quality Management; David V. Showers, *Production Manager*; Lewis R. Bassford, *Production Project Manager*; Kathie Cirucci, Timothy H. Ewing, *Senior Production Assistants*; Kevin Heubusch, *Production Assistant*; Carol R. Curtis, *Senior Production Staff Assistant*

STAFF ASSISTANTS: Aimée L. Brown, Catherine G. Cruz, Marisa Farabelli, Mary Elizabeth House, Rebecca A. Hutton, Karen A. Katz, Lisa A. LaFuria, Eliza C. Morton, Dru Stancampiano

MARKET RESEARCH: Joseph S. Fowler, Carrla L. Holmes, Marla Lewis, Joseph Roccanova, Donna R. Schoeller, Marsha Sussman, Judy T. Guerrieri

INDEX: George I. Burneston III

Composition for EXPLORING YOUR SOLAR SYSTEM by the Typographic section of National Geographic Production Services, Pre-Press Division. Type mechanicals by Carrie A. Edwards. Printed and bound by R. R. Donnelley & Sons, Chicago, Illinois. Film preparation by Catharine Cooke Studio, Inc., New York, N.Y. Color separations by Lanman–Progressive Co., Washington, D. C.; Lincoln Graphics, Inc., Cherry Hill, N.J.; and Graphic Art Service, Inc., Nashville, Tenn. Cover printed by Federated Lithographers–Printers, Inc., Providence, R.I. Teacher's Guide printed by McCollum Press, Inc., Rockville, Md.